Here's what people are saying about
The Spiral of Healing:

"Combining movement and imagery allows us to access the unconscious, resulting in a very powerful healing process. This is wonderful work!"
Jan Nilsen, Nurse Practitioner, MFT

"In three years of working with Meagan's Spiral of Healing I went from a conceptual understanding of the power of imagery in expressing and revealing deep, sometimes unconscious inner truths to living those truths in a real, integrated way. All the ages of my being were given voice and value, which inspires me daily in the present."
Suzanne Sherman, Writing Consultant &
Memoir Instructor

"The Spiral of Healing has helped me move through recent traumatic life events (the death of both my parents, the end of a long term relationship, and breast cancer). My general experience of life has changed from being a victim to discovering what I am passionate about in my life and creating what I want. The entire process has helped me become more present and alive."
Marlene Lennon, RN, MSN, FNP

"I came to the Spiral traumatized and in despair. Our probing work together allowed my grief to take a shape and find completion. This made room for other things to grow. I feel the deepest possible gratitude for an experience that has truly spiraled me into joy."
Bill Haigwood, Photojournalist, Counselor

'For me the Spiral of Healing was a powerful process of soul retrieval, which had a significant and positive impact on my life and being . . . a developmental journey on which I reclaimed and healed many lost parts, finding greater wholeness, understanding, strength, and purpose. I highly recommend this journey to anyone interested and willing to heal and get to know themselves on a much deeper level.'
Sjoukje Dekker, artist & priest

"Meagan's work engages individuals in an authentic experience that returns them to a natural state of balance and profound awareness of sel empowerment."
Kaylin Noblin, Art Therapist, MFT

"The Spiral of Healing afforded me the opportunity to explore areas of my life for growth in a safe manner. Doing the art enlivened the process, offering me the opportunity to release and heal not one time but in the manner of a spiral. Knowing that the spiral is the method freed me from judgments about areas that were crying out for growth."
Nancy Marsden, LCSW

THE SPIRAL OF HEALING

Heather—

Enjoy!

Meag

THE SPIRAL OF HEALING

A JOURNEY THROUGH THE CHAKRAS TO AWAKEN YOUR CREATIVITY AND BODY WISDOM

Meagan J. Pugh

Library of Congress Control Number: 2010918747
ISBN: Hardcover 978-1-4568-3460-9
Softcover 978-1-4568-3459-3
Ebook 978-1-4568-3461-6

This book was printed in the United States of America.

To order additional copies of this book, contact:
Xlibris Corporation
1-888-795-4274
www.Xlibris.com
Orders@Xlibris.com
88338

Contents

Acknowledgments

It is impossible to heal and grow through life without a lot of help. I am so blessed and cannot ever express in words my gratitude for all the love and support I have received. I am grateful to the Bodhi sisters—Kaylin Noblin, Leslie King, Sally Churgel, and Sally Criss and to Liana Kornfield, who have been steadfast in their love and support for my journey. Special thanks goes to the faculty of the University of Creation Spirituality for the opportunity to "reinvent" my work and create the first manuscript of the book. I am grateful to Angeles Arrien, Peter Levine, Carolyn Myss, Gabrielle Roth, Matthew Fox, and the faculty and board of the Center for the Creative Arts Therapies for their influences and focused attention to awakening consciousness.

There are many people who have helped me in the manifestation of this book, and I give thanks for Victoria Temple, Suzanne Sherman, Judy von Alten, Jenica Pugh, Connie Berens, and the staff at Xlibris.

There is no way I could be living the rich and flourishing life I lead without the continual and unswerving dedication and love of my partner, Gordon Pugh, and my children, Jenica and Emily. They are my rock and the reason I do what I do. I want to acknowledge and appreciate all the people who have trusted me with their sacred journeys, allowing me to guide and witness the awesome nature of healing and the joy that is experienced when we connect to life around us. My clients are amazing people, and I am so grateful to have been taught so much by them. A special note of thanks goes to all those who have traveled through my Spiral groups, where I have spent the last ten years developing the processes and the thoughts in this book. I have learned so much from you.

Finally, I must bow humbly before my greatest support, which is my embodied faith in the creative life force I call Spirit. Without a living, breathing, moving, and flowing connection to Spirit, my life would be hollow and without purpose. I only hope that this book and my work can be a reflection of the love and guidance I have received and am continuing to receive. Life is truly a blessing, and I will spend the rest of my days in gratitude and in service.

May the roots of your life be nourished,
May your passions awaken and thrive.
May your power be balanced with justice,
May your heart be joyful and wise.
May your voice be true and compassionate,
May your vision be focused and clear.
May you learn to guide others with wisdom and love,
And trust Beauty, Spirit, and Grace with no fear.

Preface

I want to know if you know how to melt
Into that fierce heat of living,
Falling towards the center of your longing.
I want to know if you are willing to live, day by day
With the consequence of love and the bitter unwanted passion
Of your sure defeat.
I have been told, in that fierce embrace,
Even the gods speak of God.
—David Whyte

While living in a spiritual community some thirty years ago, I experienced a dramatic turning point in my life, which came in the form of a dream. It was the impetus for my healing and my chosen career. In the dream, I was walking on a desert plain with many hundreds of people. Everyone wandering looked very tired. A father nearby told his young daughter to stay awake as sleep could bring death. I noticed a gaseous substance around my calves.

To my left, I could see that not too far away, a path led up to a hill; and at the top of that hill, there was a large cave. I made my way to the path, noticing that the people walking up and down the path were stopping to rest. I was interested and watched to make sure they got up again. Those on the path encouraged me to keep going, and I did. I climbed the hill and looked down to see thousands of people, heads tilted down, walking and helping their loved ones to keep going. It seemed strange that no one else appeared to see the path that I had seen.

Ahead, at the cave, I found cots for sleeping, a kitchen, and some people gathered toward the back, listening to someone who turned out to be my spiritual teacher. Some people were waking, and I lay down on a cot to rest. Afterwards, I took some food and water and wandered over to the group, sitting with my teacher. He welcomed me and was delighted I had come. He told me about the people on the desert. Everyone is walking through life, he explained; everyone is trying to keep going. We are tired, we need rest, but we don't think we can take it. We think it is dangerous to stop doing what we have been taught to do. Occasionally, someone would look up and notice the path and would make his or her way up here, where we are nourished, our needs are met, and our questions answered.

We are grateful we left the desert to come up here. Because we had chosen to come to the cave, he continued, we must now go back down. We must remember the cave and be available in case someone else looks up to see the path. When they do, it is our opportunity to guide them to where they need to go. I understood at that moment that I could help others to awaken as I had done. When I woke from the dream in 1981, my course in life was set. I would teach others what I had come to know.

As a young child, I longed for love and acceptance. In adolescence, I craved recognition that I was worth knowing. In college, I yearned for connection first to a mate and then to a love that was unconditional.

My earliest experiences were those of a sense of disconnection. My coping strategies grew from my experience and fear that I would not get what I needed. Some of my early beliefs were that I was not *enough*, that I was unlovable, that I was bad just for being born. Based on these core shaming beliefs, I hesitated to take risks. I was a gifted pianist, for example, but I stopped lessons at ten years old, as soon as I began having difficulties playing. In later years, I only took courses in school I knew I could handle; I was afraid to fail. When I felt overwhelmed, I honored the strategies and did what I could—I dissociated, escaped into my head, or went numb. I used my intellect to figure out how to function and look good in the world, how to present myself well on paper, and how to hide my fears. I gained skills that supported these coping strategies. But as time went on, my attempts to hide the truth of who I was only increased my desire to know the truth. I was not entirely disconnected because I recognized that I was missing something.

Events began to change in my mid-twenties when I learned to meditate and developed a spiritual practice. Through years of this practice, I learned that I was loved and lovable and connected to a wondrous source of energy. This awareness came first as a gift from my spiritual teacher and then from awakening to the creative life force that surrounds us all. Once I woke up to my place in the cosmos, I realized that at the root of my longing was a desire for connection, first to something bigger than my personal story, which was filled with trauma and pain, and then to myself and to the vast resources within and around me.

As my healing journey continued, I discovered that the path to connecting to myself and others began within my own creative life force. Through the vehicle of creativity, I came to know myself, and for the first time in my life, I came to truly know joy. Though it was difficult at times, I persevered and acknowledged my blessings, my talents, and my feelings, which included pain. By opening to it all, I opened to the astonishing beauty that exists in this life.

Over the next twenty years, I studied, healed, and lived the spiral path and created a series of art and movement processes that together form the *The Spiral of Healing* training that is the foundation of this book.

My own healing journey has been a spiraling and nonlinear path. I passed again and again through awe and desperation, deaths and rebirths, to claim resources and support that allowed me to write a different story from that into which I was born. I expanded that story to include a chosen family and community and to live a different consciousness that sees possibilities. On this spiral of healing, I reconnected to my body and came to understand how it teaches and guides me. Now I have a more accurate sense of myself (my strengths and challenges) and have gained confidence in my ability to relate to nature and to the universe. I have more compassion for myself and for all life on Earth. With this sense of compassion, I am better able to choose how I respond to life experiences, and I have more available energy to work for the greater good of all. Compassion too has improved my ability to care for myself.

THE SPIRAL OF HEALING

In 2001, I began offering the yearlong training *The Spiral of Healing*, whose processes are the basis of this book. In this book—which can take a year to complete—you will find a series of creative exercises—movements, visualizations, art explorations, and writing assignments—that have connected me and hundreds of others to a sense of wholeness. You will discover internal and external resources and use them to help you overcome past traumas. You will learn about the chakras or energy centers of the body and their effect on your sense of emotional, physical, and spiritual well-being. Chapter by chapter, you will be guided through your developmental journey as you proceed from the root chakra through to the crown or seventh chakra. See the chapter "How to Use this Book" for ways to use these processes over time.

You will encounter archetypal or universal energies as well as the many normal and healthy parts we all have living within us that are significant aspects of *The Spiral of Healing*. In becoming aware of your inner "cast of characters" (the many parts within), you will learn their useful purpose and discover how to work with them. The child archetype is one example. She (or he) is alive and well in all of us, no matter our age. But we have a choice as to how much the child in us gets to affect our life. You will learn to recognize and respect when the "little one" is communicating a thought or feeling like fear, and you will not have to identify completely with him or her. You will be able to look to a healthy adult voice within to help contain those youth fears. When we do not know how to do this, we are less likely to self-soothe and view a situation from a more realistic perspective. We are left to make choices that can be self-destructive or otherwise harmful to ourselves and others.

Through *The Spiral of Healing,* you will learn how your body and mind work together and, in particular, how the nervous system affects thoughts, emotions, and spiritual experience. Our bodies inform and support us everywhere we go. You can learn to listen to your body and recognize that it speaks in sensations such as a tightening in the belly when you feel afraid. When you have internalized a sense of safety and no longer feel you have to rely on others to provide it, you are better able to participate in life more fully and take more risks.

When we feel pain, we often split our awareness and disconnect from our bodies. To experience wholeness, we have to learn to appreciate our bodies as the container of our awareness, our range of feelings, imagination, and sensations. When we recognize and hold our bodies as sacred, we are better positioned to break through the old story of disconnection and come into a new story of unity with ourselves. When we reclaim our bodies as the sacred temples they are, we enter into an ongoing relationship between our body, heart, mind, and spirit. *The Spiral of Healing* encourages this and provides an opportunity for exploration and practice.

When we sense our body, mind, and spirit working together, we can envision a new way of being in life. Our imagination is a gift and a useful tool. We can use it to dream up something beyond what we already know, picture it, and then work to manifest it. In creating a new story, it is particularly powerful to let ourselves cultivate our senses to make room for those dreams to become reality. But sensation requires that we connect our awareness with our body, which means rewriting the old story of body as evil, sinful, or unspiritual. We must get to know our unique forms inside and out to come into the right relationship with them. Each of the creative arts processes in this book begins with a movement exercise to help ground and connect us in our bodies. The guided visualizations that follow connect our sensations with our creative imaginations.

The main objective of this book is healing on all levels—personally, collectively, and globally. This healing requires trust in life's mysteries and asks that we welcome all experiences as teachers in the infinite journey of awakening consciousness and expanded awareness.

I am convinced that the way through these troubled times is for each of us to release our creativity instead of focusing on the negative around us. There is much potential for the joy to be found there. I am excited by the possibility that when we touch into our joy, the whole world benefits. We can have an effect on our communities and the wider world around us. Theologian Frederick Buechner described it this way: "The place God calls you to be is the place where your deep gladness and the world's deep hunger meet." It is my hope that this book helps nourish your soul and inspires you to embody life to the fullest as you, your community, and the world around you experience *The Spiral of Healing*.

PART I

BEGINNING THE SPIRAL OF HEALING

INTRODUCTION

Whereas moral courage is the fighting of wrongs,
creative courage is the discovering of new forms,
new symbols, new patterns on which
a new (consciousness) society can be built.
—*Rollo May*

How do we recognize our personal and collective need to change and grow? If our eyes and hearts are open, we see many clues that we have lost our way. Within ourselves, we battle between the need to belong and our desire to express our uniqueness. We admire our individuality, yet are often shunned for our deviations from the social norm. We hope for love and unity with family members yet often feel separate and different. We long for connection in our communities yet practice isolation because we fear difference and diversity. As a culture, old ideals drive us, as well as the increasing needs of the present and future. We live in a world that espouses peace but practices war. Our collective awareness rarely questions the suppositions upon which we live our lives and make our decisions. Our cultural story, a myth that we believe is true, affects us all.

You are about to embark on a transformative healing journey. With this practical, multifaceted guide, you will begin traversing the landscape of your body, mind, emotions, and spirit through creativity and body wisdom. This book supports the journey of awakening to health and wholeness in a fun and enlivening way using creative hands-on experiences that incorporate movement, music, visualization, art, writing, and cognitive learning to bridge head and heart, logic and imagination.

The Spiral of Healing presents a process of discovery. Concepts and ideas will be introduced, explored, and repeated in various ways, representing the experience of healing and living. In other words, you have experiences, you grow from them, you return in part to where you've been/what you know, and you grow more, moving forward again. It's what I call the human spiral walk. Most of the processes center around rebuilding a healthy relationship with one's body and reclaiming lost archetypal energies due to traumatic experiences. I've included many examples of body and archetypal exercises to aid you as you journey toward wholeness and healing. Through words, movement, and creative art processes, you will experience how each chakra (energy center of the body) holds both wounding and healing. You will discover how resources like healthy boundaries, inner confidence, archetypal energies, and faith help you contain your anxieties and past experiences and support the healing of old trauma stored in your cellular tissue. Finally, you will create a new relationship with your body by paying attention to your sensations and exploring without judgment what you feel.

We are capable of healing from traumatic experiences, whether they are incident-oriented or developmental (ongoing, less identifiable, such as growing up with an emotionally absent or controlling parent). We are also capable of discovering and living by our authentic nature. Just as the acorn seed knows how to become the oak tree, so do we, as living beings, have the inherent ability to become who we truly are. We just need a little help.

In this book, you will learn about the nature of transformative healing—how it travels a spiraling rather than a linear path—and you'll learn how to navigate it and benefit by its every turn. You will access internal and external resources, create a dependable sense of safety, establish necessary boundaries, and create healthy sources of protection. You will prepare and strengthen your awareness of and relationship to your body, and you will journey into your body to retrieve and remember aspects of yourself. You will discover and begin to integrate parts of yourself that have been buried, disconnected, or otherwise set aside. As you retrieve and integrate these aspects of yourself, you will become aware of options and be able to make more satisfying choices when you face challenges in your life.

As living, breathing organisms, we respond to various kinds of stimuli—auditory, kinesthetic (sensory), and visual. The more we are aware of how we respond, the better we can begin to unravel the threads of the old stories that bind us and weave a new fabric of creativity and vitality. As you practice the exercises chapter by chapter, notice how your body responds to the information and ideas. Be aware of your breathing. Your body is as essential a part of this healing journey as your mind.

We are born as one big bag of need—as dependent creatures requiring unity, comfort, recognition, love, touch, and mirroring for our well-being. And there we are, in separate bodies surrounded by people with whom we can barely communicate. Some believe that birth itself is our first traumatic experience, the separation from a state of oneness, and that we filter all subsequent experiences through this initial trauma. Whether that trauma cripples or simply challenges us to grow depends on how we are held emotionally and physically at the time of our birth and in our early years.

All traumas impact us until we heal from them. But the way we are treated during and directly after a traumatic event has a significant effect on us. Experience creates sensation, which in turn creates feelings that lead to beliefs, thoughts, and attitudes. If a trauma is not healed by the time we reach adulthood, patterns are set, our core beliefs are established, and we feel limited in the life choices available to us.

The Spiral of Healing is the vehicle through which I healed my feelings of separation. I opened blocked and disconnected chakra energy (sensuality and communication) and retrieved the parts of myself that had been exiled from my awareness (childhood experiences). I learned to release the negative archetypal energies (judgment and control) that resulted from my early traumas. Through this process, I have been able to review, reframe, shift, and transform the coping strategies I used as a child to survive the experiences that created and reinforced my sense of separation.

CHAKRAS AND THEIR ROLES IN HEALING

The wisdom of the chakras gives us tangible ways to identify, heal, and develop our connection to body, mind, and spirit. Our chakras are part of an overall energy system. Each of the seven areas—root, sacral, solar plexus, heart, throat, brow and crown—reflects a developmental stage or life issue, a sacred truth or right to reclaim, or a particular archetype to be activated. Each chapter of Part Two goes into greater detail about the chakras and archetypes. Together, they act as a map to follow as we grow and heal. Each chakra affects the way thoughts, emotions, body, creativity, and spirit interact with each other to support the full use of energy in that area.

Our issues *and* our healing reside in the body. Our bodies can show us the areas we need to work on as well as help us heal from past experiences. For example, let's consider self-expression. If we're given permission as children to speak up, we'll have easier access to expressing ourselves as adults. If we've been hurt/shamed/abused/neglected as children, our ability to communicate any truth will feel especially difficult or scary. By focusing on opening our throat chakra, we can retrieve our ability to communicate our truth and change our experience. By expressing our truth, we can overcome our fear from early trauma and release constriction in our throat.

Through creative arts processes, we unify body, mind, and spirit to create wholeness and balance. For example, when we practice saying "no" and "yes" in a mirror or with a partner, we allow ourselves to feel the fears and courage it takes to speak out. We then create art that expresses those feelings and find what might support us to be clearer in our communications.

Because of my early traumas, I knew that life was difficult. I was disillusioned (I could not count on my parents for my safety) long before I was developmentally ready to experience that life was full of both hardships and blessings and that I could learn to navigate these ups and downs. Because of this, I longed for another reality, for something beyond the painful illusion of my life.

Led by my longing and pain, I began my healing journey—my search for what was missing—in the seventh chakra, because I knew I needed to connect to something greater than my personal world and to something more loving. It was easier for me to connect to an idea of a spiritual entity because it was a concept, not a relationship, and relationships were a place of pain for me. Over time, my attempt to connect spiritually became tangible and real, as did my connection to a spiritual community that supported my practice and gave me a positive sense of family and an avenue to begin to heal my early wounds.

FIVE KEY ELEMENTS OF THE SPIRAL

1. *The Journey of Life Must Be Embodied*

Throughout our lives, there is one constant: our embodied consciousness. Every experience we've had is recorded in our cells. And even here we battle. Our bodies become the enemy with pain or illness, heartache or anxiety. Instead of seeing the body as ally and communicator extraordinaire, we use substances, distractions, and dissociation to reject and separate from ourselves. Our traumatic experiences govern us and constrict our nervous system's ability to respond as fully or as flexibly as we'd like. We feel stuck, trapped, tired, depressed, and lonely, unable to recognize that the very help we need lies in our restricted relationship with our bodies, hearts, minds, and souls.

We are products of a culture that splits our experience of life, believes in medicating symptoms rather than addressing the underlying trauma, and a culture that denies the connection between feelings and physical ailments. In such a culture, physical pain has little to do with feelings of isolation and separateness. Depression is not connected with lower back pain or heart conditions. Breaking a leg in a car accident has no bearing on a person's mental capacities or health. Driven by a fourth-century Judeo-Christian notion, our culture splits body from mind and body from spirit and devalues feelings and physical distress as a sign of weakness. If we extend this notion to encompass the Earth as a living, breathing organism, we begin to understand how humans, taught to disconnect from feelings and the body, would allow such devastation to occur to other life forms and to Earth herself.

More recently, science and medicine have begun to see a connection between mind and body, and mind and spirit. Eastern medicine treats feelings and organs as connected: it believes that emotions can trigger a physiological response and that a physiological event can cause an emotional response. Eastern culture treats people more holistically; it considers the mind and body united. *The Spiral of Healing* is similarly holistic.

2. *Archetypal Resources Support Our Emerging Selves by Expanding Imagination to Deepen Healing*

There is value in looking to universal qualities that live in each of us. These qualities, or archetypes, reside in the chakras and help identify and acknowledge the challenges we face in our journey toward wholeness. Some common archetypes that will be introduced in this book are the Child, Caregiver, Warrior, Healer, Teacher, Visionary, and Ruler. For example, we may realize there is an aspect of ourselves demanding security above passion. Is this our Child archetype taking centerstage? If we allow our child to have all the power, we may have great energy but little follow-through. If we ignore the innocent and wild aspects of the Child within, we may be safe but have little enthusiasm for life. What is the relationship between our inner Children and our inner Adults? If our Warrior is joining forces with the child, we may be continuing old survival patterns that are no longer appropriate. If our Caregiver is imbalanced, only giving to others, we will be pulled by our needs but never learn to meet them. Finally, if we are playing the Shadow Ruler, we may misuse our power with ourselves or others and never experience our own sovereignty and compassion. We will feel controlled by others, struggle to stand on our own power, and fail to manifest a balanced and harmonious life.

In each area of our body, we can rediscover helpful energies and guidance through the processes in this book. You will be guided to find specific archetypes that will support your healing. This is an example of resourcing. My first archetypal resource was my spiritual teacher, who played the role of the Good Father. As I started my healing, I turned to friends and therapists to model healthy mothering and help me recreate my inner Mother. Then I began to reintegrate with my Healthy Child. And as I continued my work, I incorporated more archetypal energy including the Warrior and the Sensual Woman, both of which appear in later chapters of this book.

3. *Creativity, Intrinsic to Life Itself, Is a Resource for Dealing with Change*

With creativity, we can re-imagine our life story. By reclaiming our creative selves—whether through dance, play, music, creating artwork by drawing, painting, sculpting, or other activities—we can rediscover love for ourselves and come to know who that self is. Creativity aids us in discovering our strengths and challenges as well as supports our ability to change what we no longer want in behavior, feeling, or attitude. Creativity is a resource for awakening to and handling whatever life brings. We cannot stop aging, illness, or loss from occurring, but we can utilize our creative impulses and imagine the best way to meet them. Being able to hold an inner or outer image of some new situation beyond what we know supports our moving toward it and increases our confidence that we can reach that goal.

4. *Individuals Heal with the Support of and Connection to Their Communities*

Collectively, we are one living, breathing organism, and we each have a great capacity to feel, sense, be self-aware, and connect deeply with all forms of life. But we seem to have lost our ability to find community. We do not always recognize our community or our function within it. It is a sociological disconnection, a breakdown of our species' cellular structure.

One's journey toward wholeness is not only for the purpose of self-satisfaction or gratification of needs. It is a courageous step in a much greater journey of connection within the human community as well as with the life that surrounds us. Becoming connected to self allows for a greater healing to occur in the collective experience. We must know, in an embodied way, that we are part of a new story, a story of life that both precedes and continues beyond our short time on Earth. We must become aware that our actions affect generations far into the future and that we can bridge the past and the future with our love, awareness, and creative will. We are the ones with the capacity to transform the planetary destruction that abounds and to use our resources and energy to renew and regenerate our collective experience with all forms of life.

The thought that "I am the tree and the tree is me" is more than a notion; it is a truth to be sensed deeply within our being. We do that by starting where we are, in the personal, with the constant awareness of the transpersonal or collective that surrounds us. In this way, we learn to integrate body, mind, emotions, and spirit with the purpose of fulfilling our collective longing for connection and assume our rightful place in service for the greater good of all.

5. *Healing Awakens Our Consciousness*

Our ability to shift consciousness, to see all sides of the whole picture, is an aspect of our Ruler archetype and is connected to our creativity and imaginal capacities. The more we embody our life's journey, the more our consciousness grows. And consciousness is a continuum: the more we embody, the more aware we become, the more capable we are to be present for ourselves and others. That is the nature and beauty of *The Spiral of Healing.*

AWAKENING TO LIFE

Our cells have an intelligence in which each one of them knows its purpose. After reproducing themselves, they know what to do and how to complete their purpose. They know what to do because they are organized into a collective community in tissues where all cells with the same function cluster together. They have relationships with other cells, and because of this communion, they can complete their purpose. If our cells have this knowledge built into them and we are at the very least the sum of our cells, we must also know that we incarnate with a purpose. We may not be awake to it, but it is living in us.

It is a gift to be awake and to know we are awake. Even more exciting, the creative process of waking up is infinite, and the power to create is divinely inspired. My intention with the practices of *The Spiral of Healing* is to ignite the process of awakening our cellular memory to whom and what we are—to become conscious by listening to our bodies and living our creativity.

This book is my contribution to awakening consciousness. When we heal from our traumatic experiences, we become present to life. Our old needs no longer drag us into the past, and fear (that we won't get what we need) doesn't drive us forward on a wayward course. We meet life as it comes.

Many traditions honor the spiritual concept of detachment, the letting go of the pull of the material world which stops us from experiencing freedom. But we first must be attached to something in order to strive for an experience of detachment. On my healing journey, I knew I needed to first bond, and I met that need by living in a spiritual community. I had no internal connection to spirit, but I had an external connection to a group that helped me feel something real besides my painful everyday life experiences. My seventh chakra opened, and I felt devotion to something greater than myself. But I still did not know who I was; I was only connected to a very small part of me.

We all have different stories and different needs, but still we start the healing journey together at the same place. It's a hero's journey, a bold step into living fully, which means facing the guards at the gate and the demons who've lived in the shadows so we can claim the jewels that are rightfully ours.

WAKING UP TO YOURSELF

CREATIVITY, IMAGINATION, AND BODY WISDOM

Creativity and imagination are not frosting on the cake:
They are integral to our sustainability . . .
They are the essence of who we are.
—Matthew Fox

I often tell clients that all roads lead to Home. What I mean by that is that we are given many opportunities to come back to ourselves. Our creativity opens the gate; it's the "open sesame," the way to the jewels hidden within. Through our creative process, we uncover the expansive truth of our experience. To connect with our own unique brand of creative flow is to bring together all of the aspects of the human experience—our thoughts, feelings, imagination, behavior or movement patterns, and body sensations. Creativity allows us to come into unity with ourselves. Without it, we tend to shrivel up and feel empty, without ability to function. We are a little more than an exquisite machine whose parts work but have little juice, little energy.

To be creative is to birth new energy, to feel our consciousness, to awaken us to our connection with life. When we are born, we leave the oneness state of the womb to become unique individuals. We spend the rest of our lives striving to get back to that experience of unity and to feel our connection rather than separation from life. What bridge our uniqueness and our oneness are two experiences: love and creativity. When we are creating, we are no longer alone because we are engaged in the creative force that is behind everything. We become a cocreator, and our sense of guidance expands. We move beyond our safety zones into the mystery. Alone, we would not go there.

Creativity is one of the platforms where, as theologian and scholar Matthew Fox describes it, "the divine and human meet."[1] When we are creating, we sense a presence of something supporting us, and we risk moving from the known to the unknown.

One of the most creative parts of ourselves is the body we live in. Even without our conscious awareness, we are flowing in cross currents of electrical, neurological, chemical, and hormonal rivers that exquisitely move in and around and through each other, interacting and creating all that we need to live. When we apply our conscious awareness, our thoughts and feelings, and, most importantly, our imagination to this multicurrent extravaganza, we find ourselves in a wonderland of sensations, images, movements, thoughts, and feelings that make up our "soma," our awareness of ourselves from the inside out.[2] When the body is objectified, as it is sometimes for medical purposes, we learn a set of information that reveals function levels and working parts of a unique creation. When we integrate our soma into the picture, we suddenly come alive and feel our fullness and richness. We are back in Aladdin's cave, and having said the magic words, we receive the jewels of our life—integration, compassion, unity—a feeling of oneness within ourselves.

BUILDING A HEALTHY RELATIONSHIP WITH YOUR BODY

Our relationship to our bodies has been impacted by our culture, history, and religious beliefs. The western medical model views the healthy human body as a well-oiled machine; when there is an accident or illness, one simply replaces parts or uses products that destroy unwanted buildup. Thoughts and emotions are considered only when they impact the results of the treatment. If, for example, someone feels depressed from the side effects of a particular medication, he or she may be given antidepressants. In this model, the body is objectified and seen as separate from mind, emotions, or spirit.

In order for true healing to begin, we have to break out of this paradigm of separation and powerlessness. The bridge between old and new paradigms sees illness or injury as an initiation or wake-up call. It invites us to journey within to discover what these experiences are here to teach us. This more holistic model invites us to embody the principle that there is no separation between mind, emotions, body, and spirit. Each is its own doorway into a total, interconnecting, breathing, living organism.

Human life is not a machine; it is a continuous journey. Experiences, including death, are teachers. The path of life is spiral, circling around and coming back to itself while moving forward at the same time. This means that in the future, we may find ourselves in similar situations we encounter now. Each time we arrive at this familiar place, we know a little more and have more tools with which to work. There is no focused goal that is "right" or "perfect." Rather, the objective is wholeness, which includes health, disease, trauma, and healing. Illness, abuse, and injury are shattering experiences that can potentially awaken our sacred dream or purpose for incarnating, for being alive.

Science is discovering that thoughts and feelings change our physiology in the same way that physiological changes produce mental and emotional responses. The neurophysiology of emotions links the unconscious mind and everything we think and feel with our bodies.[3] Experiencing a greater understanding and purpose of our life's journey helps us to construct an inner container for healing. When we are connected to the creative life force and are listening to all the aspects of who we are, we can utilize more of ourselves to heal.

To heal, we must feel safe and connected to ourselves. Safety grows from trust and experience. Without it, we feel alone and contracted. That is why it is so important to learn the language of our bodies, to retrieve the sensations of safety and comfort, and to recognize when our body is alerting us to danger. Often, our body speaks to us in the language of pain or illness. That may be the only way we are willing to listen. In this way, it acts as our ally, getting our attention and alerting us to the need for healing.

BODY AS HERO'S JOURNEY

If we regard our focus on the body as a descent into our deeper selves or as a hero's journey of recovery, then we must prepare for this adventure with certain tools. As with the early stories and ancient myths, the journeyer often begins by finding a special horse, a magic cloak, and an old man or woman (the "wise one") who offers invaluable advice. For our part, we use the imaginal process to retrieve energies that travel with us on our journey (our own special horse, magic cloak, and wise woman).

Building resources is critical for the challenges we will meet. The first resource is creating a new relationship with our body. Using our imagination and the creative process, we can find a way to feel safety, nourishment, peace, containment, and pleasure in our bodies. With our body as guide and ally, we receive the information and support we need to transform our life experiences and embrace a new consciousness of wholeness and interconnection.

THE CREATIVE ARTS THERAPIES PLAY A PART

Several key concepts in the field of the creative arts therapies have contributed to the healing process of the Spiral. Central is *relationship as the foundation for healing*. When working through the Spiral, it is important that the client and therapist (or facilitator or coach) experience their interconnectivity and act as the warp and weft of the healing tapestry. A therapist's own healing journey allows him or her to recognize and empathize with another's suffering and their potential for joy. Together, they can weave for each other an experience of wonder and growth.

Another central concept is the magic of the imagination and our inherent creativity. Through dialog process, we can learn from our imagery by connecting with our conscious mind and receiving its wisdom.[4] This requires a willingness to think outside the box, to invite in the possibility of change, and in doing so, to be childlike, even silly. Our inherent creativity supports our ability to manifest our full potential, and in doing so, we give back to our community.[5]

The third key concept is the commitment to doing our own inner work so that we can heal ourselves and then be available to guide others and then model the process of healing. By recognizing the other as our self, we are invited into an experience of depth, creativity, and wisdom.

IMAGINATION AND TRAUMA RESOLUTION

Creativity and imagination have been used in the healing of physical and emotional aftereffects of trauma for many years and in many cultures.[6] Familiar visual anchors and imaginal safe places have been used as a means to stop or slow down the process in order for the nervous system to catch up to itself.[7] Imaginal techniques aid in building inner resources, which allow one to retrieve one's full range of experience in order to resolve unpleasant memories.

A somatic approach to healing combines body wisdom with imagination and feeling. In it, we are invited to pay attention to our nervous system as the guide to releasing traumatic experiences. In a technique known as pendulation, we are asked to follow a gentle movement back and forth, between an inner resource and an experience of activation or heightened alert response, which we register as danger. When we do this simple pendulation, the nervous system reorganizes itself around new ways to respond to stress, which changes the way we think, feel, move, and imagine. If we pay attention and work with what psychologist Peter Levine calls the SIBAM Model (body sensations, imagery, behavior, affect, and meaning), we can resolve early traumatic experiences.[8] The exercises in this book offer opportunities to pay attention to these areas and deepen both experience and understanding.

Figure 1. Resources and *The Spiral of Healing*

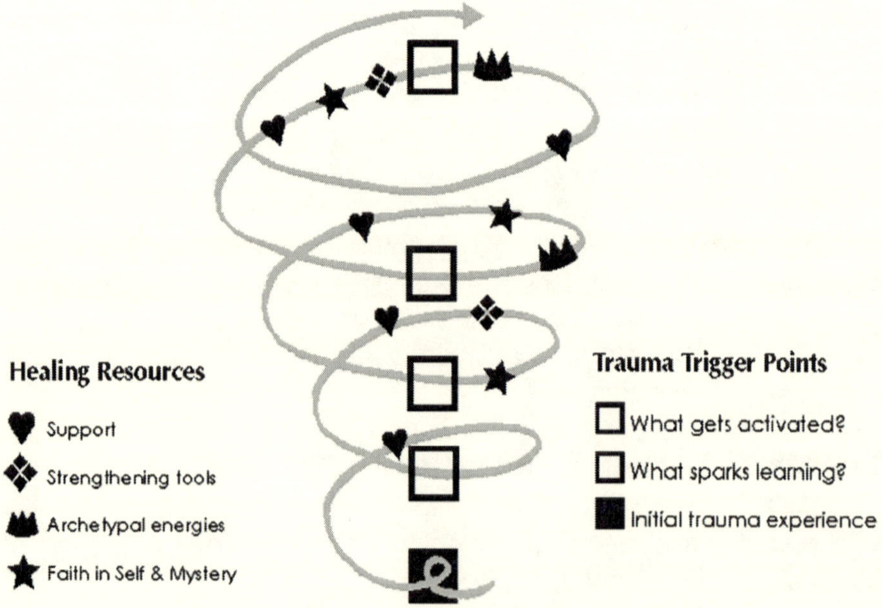

In *The Spiral of Healing*, resources are essential to offset and balance the trigger responses so common to traumatic memory. In Fig. 1 ("Resources and *The Spiral of Healing*"), trauma is represented by the black box at the base of the spiral.

The box refers to a traumatic event that is often experienced as taking over one's daily consciousness, thus filling the entire cycle of movement. As we begin to bring resources back into our awareness (e.g., support, as symbolized by the heart in the diagram), we can begin to feel more connected to our everyday life.

Resources in the healing journey include inner and outer support, strengthening tools to protect oneself, archetypal energies formerly trapped in the trauma memory, and a sense of faith in oneself and in the mystery of life. Together, these new capacities expand our options as part of the spiraling experience. The traumatic event once registered as shattering and overwhelming is then changed into another experience in a long chain of circumstances that are now resourceful. Thus, the spiral of our life expands and balances the trauma with embodied healing memory.

THE FOUR PATHS OF CREATION SPIRITUALITY

Using our imagination, creative resources and body wisdom allows us to feel that we are a part of an ongoing universal reality. Through this awareness, we come into recognition of the spiritual and cosmological foundations for healing. We remember that we are not alone, that we have strengths and allies, and that our journey spirals us into greater and greater appreciation of who we truly are. One example of this is to practice the mystical paths of Creation Spirituality[9] where we are brought into a spiral journey of transformation. Using the four paths as a guide, we can travel through most challenges and remember our blessings.

The first path in Creation Spirituality, Via Positiva, invites us to acknowledge the awe and blessings of life. We recognize the beauty and diversity within us, around us, and beyond us. We are invited to pay attention to the "other" as a gift and to question our narrow vision of right and wrong or dualistic thinking. We are grateful for our ability to commune with all life.

The second path, Via Negativa, supports our descent into the mystery where we connect with shadow, darkness, and the need to let go and be empty. We allow ourselves to sense or feel the contractions as well as the expansions and to get comfortable with silence and not knowing. We grieve, move into the places within us that are scary, uncomfortable, and unknown, and learn to let go and trust.

Via Creativa emerges from out of the first two paths, when we experience our connection to a divine creative life force. We create and cocreate our reality. We use our creativity as a means to discover our connection to all forms of life and to give birth to our cosmic relationships.

The fourth path, Via Transformativa, brings us into right relationship with compassion and justice. This is a movement from personal healing to an awareness of the suffering and joy of community and Earth systems. It furthers the awareness that "all is one[10]," and our ability to feel the pain of others enables us to make global changes on a local level. It is a state of empowerment and joy. Through inspired community, we spiral back to the Via Positiva. By having a mystical experience of awe and blessing and reverence for all of creation, we can overcome our experience of separation and come together as a sacred community working for the benefit of all life.

CHAKRAS

The Spiral of Healing, as experienced in the four paths of Creation Spirituality, is a journey toward wholeness and health. We prepare for this journey by creating safety, finding protection and inner guidance, and recognizing boundaries. As we travel into our body-mind-spirit, our map is the chakra system.

The word "chakra" is Sanskrit for wheel or disk. The chakra system, originating from the ancient yoga traditions of India, refers to spinning vortices of energy within our bodies that act together to receive, assimilate, and transmit life energies. You can think of these wheels as recording and containing programming about certain life functions.

Figure 2. Chakras

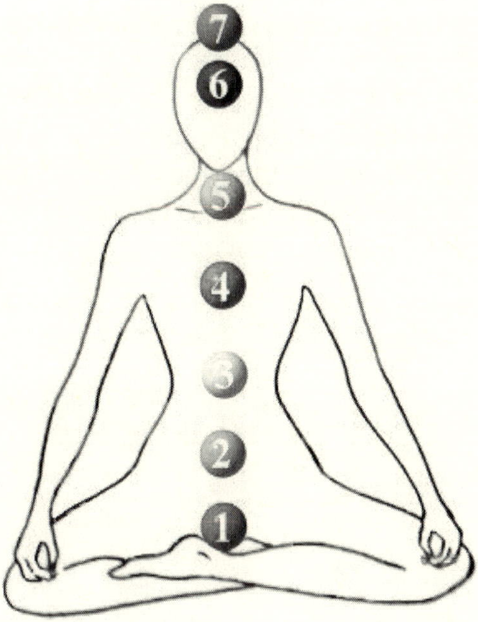

There are seven major chakras or energy centers in the body, arranged vertically from the base of the spine to the top of the head. They are (1) Root; (2) Sacral; (3) Solar Plexus; (4) Heart; (5) Throat; (6) Brow or Third Eye; and (7) Crown. These centers correspond to glands in the endocrine system, organs, and body processes such as breathing and digesting. They also correspond to the locations of high concentrations of receptor activity in our cells known as hot spots or nodal points.[11] It is through these nodal points that information in the form of thoughts, feelings, and sensations enter the body.

Psychologically, the chakras relate to major areas in our lives: survival and connection, sexuality and creativity, power and self-esteem, love and compassion, communication and will, thought and imagination, and wisdom and spirituality. Correspondingly, we can think about a basic human right in each chakra. These rights are: the right to have, the right to feel, the right to act, the right to love and be loved, the right to speak, the right to see, and the right to know.[12]

Physically, there is a connection between the chakras and health issues; in particular, certain organs, emotional issues, and physical dysfunction are often linked to each chakra. For example, the fourth chakra, heart and lungs, may point to issues of love and hatred, grief and anger, especially when physical dysfunctions as heart attacks, breast cancer, and asthma are present.

Spiritually, the chakras have been associated with seven sacred truths that act as the foundation for each of these energy centers.[13] These truths are: All is one, honor one another, honor oneself, love is divine power, surrender personal will to divine will, seek only the truth, and live in the present moment.

Figure 3. CHAKRA TABLE

	RIGHTS	**SACRED TRUTHS**	**DEVELOPMENTAL STAGES**	**LIFE ISSUES**
1	TO HAVE	ALL IS ONE	PRENATAL -3 YEARS	SECURITY
2	TO FEEL	HONOR ONE ANOTHER	EARLY CHILDHOOD	BELONGING
3	TO ACT	HONOR ONESELF	LATENCY AGE - ADOLESCENTS	IDENTITY
4	TO LOVE	LOVE IS DIVINE POWER	YOUNG ADULTHOOD	LOVE AND ACCEPTANCE
5	TO SPEAK	SURRENDER PERSONAL WILL TO DIVINE WILL	ADULTHOOD	COMPETENCY
6	TO SEE	SEEK ONLY THE TRUTH	MATURITY	PURPOSE
7	TO KNOW	LIVE IN PRESENCE	ELDERSHIP	SURRENDER

The chakras may also be read as a road map of developmental issues. As we age, we receive and store information. There is usually a connection between traumatic experiences at a certain stage and the shutting down of energy in a chakra. Likewise, where we were supported and encouraged, we will find an open and flourishing energy center. Briefly, first, second, and third chakras record experiences in utero through adolescence and relate to issues of safety, belonging, and self-esteem. Fourth chakra receives information from age three years through young adulthood and works with acceptance and identity. Fifth and sixth chakras develop from childhood through the adult years and looks at the issue of competency and power. Seventh chakra records experiences from twelve through the end of life and works with the issue of life purpose. As we cyclically repeat these stages of development throughout our lives, we can be aided by an awareness of the wisdom of the chakras and work with the related issues in our healing.

The chakra system is a complex map of the human condition. It can also be used to guide us on the healing journey as we experience physical, mental, emotional, and spiritual awakenings. As we explore each chakra, we will touch on these aspects and relate the information to our own lives. In addition, we will discover the archetypal energies that live in each chakra. It is my experience that all roads do lead to home and each chakra offers a doorway or path to our awareness and our healing.

CREATION SPIRITUALITY AND THE SEVEN CHAKRAS

It is possible to bridge body and spirit by describing the chakras as powers, potentials, and blessings that we have the right and responsibility to develop. Developing a spiritual perspective of the body is what brings together and releases healing energy for ourselves and our planet. Studying the chakras is how we, as a culture, can redeem our relationship to our bodies and to the greater body of Earth. An example of this is in the relationship Matthew Fox draws between the chakras and seven principles of Creation Spirituality.[14]

The first principle is Cosmology. In the first chakra, this is a vibration that connects an individual to the whole, grounds us to the earth, and connects us to the heavens. We are reminded to appreciate the blessings of sound and vibration in our lives.

The second principle, corresponding to the second chakra, welcomes sexuality and generativity as blessing. It is a feminist, non-dualistic philosophy committed to overcoming the separation of matter from spirit, spirituality from sexuality, and male from female. We are invited to live out a life of interconnectivity with the blessings of our sensual and sexual selves.

The third principle, relating to the Solar Plexus, is one of empowerment and liberation theology, the notion of oppressed people becoming empowered. It encourages us to have compassion and moral outrage, to work for social justice and right action and to accept the blessings of our gut reactions.

Compassion, the fourth principle, corresponds to the Heart chakra. It encourages us to use our heart energy for healing, forgiveness, and letting go of remorse. We are reminded to breathe and to welcome the blessings of our heart, immune system and defenses, and circulatory system.

The fifth principle corresponds to the Throat and supports the expression of one's truth and wisdom. It refers to the prophetic call to speak out and to interfere with what is obstructing what we deeply believe in. It invites us to find our voices, to sing, to speak praise, and to be grateful.

The sixth principle, insight, intuition, and perception, corresponds to the Brow chakra. Here, Fox places the quality of creativity and the flow of spirit in right relationship with the blessings of the mind. We are invited to study, to learn, to self-reflect, and to unite our creativity with the sacred energy of mind.

The last principle, relating to the seventh or Crown chakra, is community-building. Here, we are asked to send our light into the world for connection, to send it out to past ancestors and future descendants in order to make community happen. We are invited to gather, share, and reach out our light energy from all the chakras and extend it into relationships with other people. Then we receive the blessings of warmth, light giving and light connecting, and broadening diversity.

As we have seen, creativity, imagination, and body wisdom form the center of the healing spiral. When we combine our innate gifts of creativity and imagination with a working and loving relationship with our body, we are able to create a foundation for healing that is unparalleled. In order to awaken these gifts and our body's inherent wisdom and structure, we must learn new skills and create new resources for ourselves. These skills are physical, emotional, mental and spiritual in nature and revolve around our ability to dream and long for integration. The first skill is to ask for help. Then help is always on the way.

HOW TO USE THIS BOOK

Great Lions can find peace in a cage.
But we should only do that as a last resort.
So those bars I see that restrain your wings,
I guess you won't mind
If I pry them open.
—*Rumi*

Transformational experiences that involve movement (body) and creative process (body and mind working together) are part of the purpose of this book and the reason for taking the journey of *The Spiral of Healing*. It's the beginning of a lifelong relationship with your mind and body working together.

Through movement, imaging (using your imagination in visualization and through art process), expression, and reflection, we journey through the seven energy centers, or chakras, exploring the issues held there. Each of the creative arts processes is composed of four parts: Movement, Guided Visualization, Art, and Writing. Movement, or body awareness exercises, connect you to your body and awaken sensation and feelings. They are exercises done to the music of your choice that bring your attention to the sensation of your body and are followed by the imaginal practice of guided visualization. Guided visualization is one of the best ways to move into a more connected place within oneself. Through this practice, you use your imagination to create pictures that further guide you in your self-discovery as you move into the art process.

The art processes use a range of materials; a list of suggested materials follows. The writing is usually a form of journaling about the experience, which deepens understanding and integration. For this, you'll need a lined or unlined journal or other writing notebook of whatever size appeals to you, and a favorite pen or pencil.

The flow of chakras is not linear; however, in this book, the chakras follow a linear path for ease of understanding of the process. You can open this book to any chapter and use the creative arts processes there, but it's best to read the chapters and do the exercises in order the first time through as each chapter and each process builds on the one before it. Later, you can make your own connections between issues and chakras and return to chapters as desired for further exploration. For example, because of the connection between early experiences and core beliefs, if you are working on early abandonment issues, you might like to return to Chapter One and then go on to Chapter Six to go in more deeply. Each chapter will suggest any connections with other chapters. At the end of each chapter, questions to ponder and further exercises are offered to deepen your experience and help you connect to the information in the chapter. This allows you to carry the creative process into additional writing and even dreaming before you continue with the next chapter. It is helpful to allow yourself ample time to process the information and the experiences in each chapter. There is no hurry. You can take a month on each chapter, for example, or go through the entire spiral once and then return to the beginning and start again. Find the rhythm that works for you.

CREATING SACRED SPACE

Preparing your space for the creative arts processes is essential to creating a healing experience. A quiet, respectful atmosphere will allow you to focus entirely on yourself. Make sure you are not interrupted by telephone or by other people. Before you begin a creative process, try lighting a candle and thinking of friends, family, anyone who loves and cares for you and call them into the space to act as witness and protection. Sit quietly for a few minutes and breathe deeply as a means of centering yourself. Make sure you have enough room to move your body in the movement exercise, you have your art supplies and workspace , and your journal or other writing notebook on hand.

PREPARING TO ENGAGE YOUR BODY

You need to be prepared for the adventure that awaits you in revitalizing your relationship with your body. For your well-being and sense of safety, you do not want to move too quickly, go too deep too fast. You want to build your connection to your body in a healthy, uplifting way. When you combine movement and imaging working with the body and creative process, you bypass defenses and resistance, which can bring up experiences quickly. That is why it is especially important to do some preparation. Section Four, "Help Is on the Way," gives more ideas for resources and strengthening tools for the journey.

For the movement exercises, wear comfortable, loose clothing you won't mind getting dirty during the art process. Have a tape player or CD player available for music, which is recommend for all movement exercises, and for playing movement instructions and guided visualizations from *The Spiral of Healing* CD. If you are working in a group, have someone read the movement instructions and visualizations for the others to follow or use *The Spiral of Healing* CD. Be sure to speak slowly and give plenty of time for the instructions to be followed. Once the visualization is finished, move directly into the art process with as little interruption as possible.

BODY AWARENESS EXERCISE

Here is an example of a body awareness exercise. It is designed to show how your sensations, thoughts, feelings, and movements are connected.

> Notice one sensation anywhere in your body (such as heaviness, throbbing, pressure, or dullness) . . . As you pay curious and nonjudgmental attention to this sensation, what thoughts pop into your mind? Where do you sense those thoughts, and how does your body hold them?
>
> How do you feel focusing on this sensation, and where do you feel it? How could you move your body to show this thought or feeling? As you pay more attention, what image(s) come to mind and how can you show part of that image in movement?
>
> If you could find an opposite image, thought, or feeling than the ones you have connected with the difficult sensation,

what would it/they be? Sense those in your body as well . . . Play with going back and forth between the difficult and opposite and notice what changes in your sensations . . .

Write your experiences in a journal.

ART PROCESSES

Allow yourself plenty of time for the art processes—thirty to sixty minutes. If you have more time, go for it. Art process is both meditative and transformative in the doing. Creating art allows your right brain to speak to your more linear self in symbols, which you can later understand with your rational mind.

Begin the art process with an open mind; trying to draw an idea can be frustrating. Allow yourself to be guided by the materials and your feelings from the visualization and movement; they can bring you new awareness. Notice how you feel as you approach the art materials. You may be drawn to creating a collage with found images this time; in the next process, you may feel like filling a large piece of paper with images you create by hand.

With all art processes, remember that it is about the *process* not the product. You do not have to color within the lines. There is no one to impress. You are free to be wild with color, with mixing media, with making huge shapes and images or very small ones. You may like to make a box and put things in it that are symbolic to you, and only you will know they are in there. The thoughts and feelings coming through when you are creating are part of the process. Notice them. When it's time to write about the experience, you can record these and other thoughts. It's all part of the journey.

Materials themselves can aid in the art process. For instance, if you are feeling contracted and rigid, using watercolors or clay will move you into a more fluid place. If you are feeling ungrounded and spacey, colored pencils and collage materials can help you feel more anchored. Always check in with yourself before you begin a process.

Art process can be a messy experience. If you don't have a space you are comfortable with getting messy, use plastic sheeting or drop cloths on the floor or furniture so you feel more at ease.

It is also important to have choices in your art materials. Each art process will include a list of ideas for art supplies if there are recommended ones, but there are some basics to have on hand.

ART MATERIALS

- Large white paper (18 x 24), loose or a pad
- Oil pastels, chalk pastels, and/or colored pencils
- Watercolor or tempera paints and brushes
- Magazines, old calendars, greeting cards, and other found images of nature, animals, people, and spiritual symbols for collage
- Assorted colored construction paper
- White glue, hot glue, and hot glue gun
- Clay, grey or terra cotta (comes in twenty-five-pound bags)
- Assorted fabrics in various colors and textures
- Sparkly materials like jewels, beads, glitter, shiny paper, pipe cleaners
- Natural items such as sticks, shells, rocks, crystals, driftwood, sand, silk flowers
- Cardboard pieces in sixteen-inch rounds and rectangles
- Blank muslin doll forms, eleven inches and smaller (see Art Materials Resources)
- Mask-making materials—plaster gauze in rolls
- Scissors

Allow yourself to experiment with new materials along with those you already know.

DIALOGING WITH THE IMAGE

When you feel completed in the art process, allow yourself time to communicate, or dialog, with the image itself. Assume the image is an entity that has come to you as a gift to teach you more about yourself. With paper and pencil and your dominant hand (your right hand if you're right-handed), welcome the image and ask it why it has come or what it is about, even if you think you know. Allow the answers to enter your imagination and write them with your non-dominant hand. Usually, this happens in larger print or incomplete sentences and may not always make sense. Continue the dialog process until there is some resolution or you wish to stop. Remember that imagery is a gift from your unconscious self and can open up new doorways into building a healthy relationship with yourself and your body. If it is not already a part of the writing exercise, try it out once you've completed the art.

USING THIS FORMAT IN A GROUP

The processes offered in this book were developed in a group format with a trained art therapy facilitator. This book is offered as a resource for other group leaders to use as a way to supplement and support their work. It can also be used in a non-facilitated group with rotating leadership or no leader. With no leader, it is essential to use pretaped movement and visualization exercises so everyone can participate. In a led group, one person can read the exercises for the others. It is important to allow plenty of time for the process and for sharing.

We need each other and community in order to heal. The circle approach to healing consists of individuals receiving and giving to each other and deepening wisdom through shared experience. When we work together, bringing forth our issues and wisdom, we strengthen the collective. By sharing our creativity in a safe and sacred container, we empower others and ourselves to step beyond trauma and alienation into a community of respect and compassion.

When sharing artwork, some suggested guidelines are offered.

First, it is important to remember that one's images are sacred and belong to the artist. In sharing those images, others may therefore accept the sharing but offer no interpretation. This allows for the person sharing to speak his or her feelings and thoughts in a safe place without judgment. If feedback is desired, it is important for others in the group to own their projections (e.g., When I see your image, I feel sad/angry/happy because . . . [personal sharing]). This allows the artist to listen without having to accept someone else's experience as his or her own reality. To project one's own interpretation on another's image does not allow enough room for the artist's own experience of the creative process and can be felt as discounting or judgmental.

Second, it is important that each person in the group get equal time to speak. Someone must act as timekeeper in order to keep the space safe and sacred. Third, I suggest that groups open and close with a simple ritual that welcomes in spiritual guidance and protection, perhaps connected with Earth energies, and calls in qualities needed to be present in the circle. This deepens the energy of the circle and establishes the container for the processes.

HELP IS ON THE WAY

RECLAIMING RESOURCES AND STRENGTHENING TOOLS

What fortitude the Soul contains,
That it can so endure
The accent of a coming Foot,
The opening of a Door!
—Emily Dickinson

To walk *The Spiral of Healing,* we embrace four primary resources: internal and external support, archetypal energies, strengthening tools, and faith in ourselves and in the mystery of the universe.

Support is essential to counteracting pervasive feelings of isolation and separation, common aftereffects of trauma, and the result of a society that reveres individuality and self-reliance. We need community, friends, family, and others who can listen to us and guide our path of awakening. The creative process of the Spiral begins as an external support. It enhances our reliance on inner resources. Along the way, it is helpful to develop skills for listening to inner guidance. This builds inner support. Disciplines that lead into stillness and a sense of connection with all life, such as meditating or simply walking or sitting quietly in locations where you feel safe and at ease, are wonderful ways to practice listening. It is also helpful to practice being as present as possible. Thoughts of disturbing past experiences or fear-based future projection can be anxiety-producing and is not supportive or self-nurturing.

To enjoy a full and rich life experience, we have to reclaim the ability to protect ourselves, to integrate all of the parts of ourselves, and to explore and heal ourselves. In the Spiral, through the imaginal practices of guided visualization followed by visual imaging through art, we access the energy that resides in our unconscious and retrieve inner strengths and talents and other aspects of ourselves that have been temporarily lost due to trauma. This energy expresses itself in the form of archetypes that we can recognize and name. You may already be familiar with some of the most common ones: the Ruler, Visionary, Teacher, Healer, Warrior, Lover, and Child.

What do you retrieve when you access the archetype of the Child? Often, it is a sense of wonder, delight, and playfulness. In the Lover, you may connect to passion and creativity. In the Warrior, you find your strength, protection, and clarity. In the Healer, there is an opportunity for self-nurturing. The Teacher gives us a chance to retrieve the courage to speak our truth. The Visionary offers us a chance to expand our ability to set and achieve goals. In the Ruler, we remember how to steward our power in balance with our total being.

Creative exercises in this chapter and throughout the book will help you access and recognize the roles your archetypes play so you can use them to your benefit. Through the creative exercises, you'll also develop tools for self-strengthening and learn about necessary boundaries. Boundaries begin with discerning what is or isn't needed at any time. This can include saying no when you need to and recognizing and effectively communicating your needs and feelings. In the boundaries exercises at the end of this chapter, you'll learn to identify and set boundaries, practice healthy defensive responses, and discover how to manage reactivity.

To feel empowered and capable, we have to trust ourselves and others. We can learn to achieve this by gaining tools for supporting and expressing our true nature. Our self-esteem grows as we learn to let go of old ways and build trust in our ability to learn the next lesson and put it to good use in our lives. This leads to a sense of empowerment and to an expanded awareness of our life purpose. As our self-esteem grows, so does our trust in others, and we are better able to open to a heartening experience of universal support.

Living authentically walks hand in hand with effort and faith. It is a gift, and it is our birthright.

GETTING STARTED

At the start of any journey of self-discovery, it is helpful to know where you are at the present moment. The first creative process, the Self-Portrait, gives you an opportunity to imaginally experience how you perceive yourself right now. It will be a valuable marker of your progress.

Also important at the outset is developing a healthy working relationship with your body. In our everyday lives, we tend not to pay attention to our body unless it hurts or doesn't measure up to cultural standards. We attempt to fix, change, or medicate to avoid pain or numb. I suggest a new approach. What if we viewed our body as our ally and understood that it sometimes communicates its needs through pain? What if the sensations we feel are our body's way of alerting us to something profound?

Creating a loving, working relationship with your body—feeling all there is to feel—can support your confidence and help you build mastery in whatever you choose to accomplish. Throughout this journey, we will support our new relationship with our body (our body is our ally) by practicing feeling the connection between our thoughts, feelings, images, and sensations.

BUILDING RESOURCES

When we are traumatized as children, we tend to lose any sense of boundary and protection. We may feel abandoned by the adults around us. To combat the pain of this experience, we find ways, with our limited understanding and with the help of one aspect of the inner Warrior, to create a strategy for protecting ourselves.

One of the jobs we give our immature Warrior involves dissociation—leaving our bodies. By numbing out parts of ourselves, we abandon our feelings to become the good girl or boy or to become better able to take care of those around us who seem to need help. This is a creative solution to an unsafe situation. But what works in childhood can become a stumbling block in adulthood because the job of protection is in the hands of the child; and as the child, we cannot care for ourselves appropriately as adults. Through the creative process of shield-making, later in this chapter, we fully assume responsibility for this aspect of our life—we are the adult at the same time we support our inner child to feel safe and become the child again, this time creating a protection that is imagistic and perennially powerful.

Drawing clear boundaries enhances our feeling of personal safety and builds inner strength. Healthy boundaries help us sense danger before we're hurt and help us keep unwarranted energy from coming our way. They also help us respect other people's boundaries.

To know our boundaries is to know our energy field—where we end and others begin. This is a developmental task, something perceived bodily through the process of separation in early childhood. When we are very young, until we have our own boundaries, we need someone to provide them for us, usually parents and teachers. We feel secure when we know the rules, as long as they are not oppressive. As we mature and become more autonomous, the boundaries that once made us feel safe can be eased.

In healthy development, a child is encouraged to separate from his or her mother when he or she is ready to become age-appropriately autonomous, somewhere between three and four years of age. Development of this level of autonomy, however, can be a challenging task for child *and* parent. A parent can, for instance, be uncomfortable dealing with a needy child and can speed up the process of separation, requiring that the child take care of himself. When this happens, a child becomes independent too early and does not develop a sense of trust that she or he is safe to explore or have needs. In addition, the concept of "autopoesis," or the ability to become oneself, is inhibited. An example is the child who may feel insecure about learning to ride a bike. If he or she is expected to learn without falling or needing comfort, he or she may learn to ride the bike anyway but will stifle his or her feelings of vulnerability and pain.

And there are other ways a child's healthy individuation can be inhibited during development. A parent's—or a child's—fears of autonomy, for example, can keep him or her dependent on the parent. Without the cues needed to feel competent, the child becomes insecure and fearful. Another common issue is a parent's inattention, which can be particularly harmful during this critical age period. Without the sense of a safety net for the risky task of separation, a child can feel fear or shame when she follows her biological movement toward autonomy. All of these scenarios lead to confusion about boundaries and the underdevelopment of intuition and instinct.

Until we know where we end and others begin, we cannot act appropriately in the world. We cannot trust that what we sense is true for us, and we cannot act upon that sense for protection. Without clear boundaries, we may believe, rightly or wrongly, that we are being held prisoner by someone or something or that if we claim our boundaries, we will be attacked or abandoned.

In the archetypal realm, personal boundaries and issues of self-protection express the warrior/leader in us. In classical times, warriors carried the shield of their land, which symbolized the protection of the kingdom. To connect with our own warrior energy is to align with compassion, clarity, truth-telling, and conscious action. It is to know ourselves and our capacities and to have a working instinctual defensive response to danger. This natural ability to access our defensive orienting responses of flight or fight allows us to avoid danger and defend ourselves. When we are reconnected to this, we no longer need to lash out or hurt others or ourselves.[1] The skills of a Warrior include presence, honor, respect for all things, judicious communication, an ability to set limits and boundaries, responsibility and discipline, and ability to demonstrate the right use of power.[2] We will explore the Warrior archetype in more depth later.

In preparing for the journey into the body, we need to enhance our experience of boundaries. Through movement and the creative arts, we will call this energy to us. Below is a list of the signs of healthy boundaries. Refer to this list as you practice the exercises in this chapter.

SIGNS OF HEALTHY BOUNDARIES

1. Having appropriate trust—you reveal a little of yourself at a time then check to see how the other person responds to your sharing. You decide whether a potential relationship will be good for you.
2. Maintaining personal values and not surrendering them when under pressure by others to do so. Defining your truth and knowing who you are and what you want.

3. Trusting your own decisions.
4. Clearly communicating your wants and needs while understanding that you may not always have those wants and needs met.
5. Weighing consequences before acting on sexual impulse, being sexual when you want to be, experiencing your own pleasure instead of monitoring your partner's reactions as a gauge for your pleasure.
6. Saying no to food, gifts, touch, and sex when you don't want them.
7. Noticing when others display inappropriate boundaries, noticing when someone invades your boundaries.
8. Becoming your own loving parent. Talking to yourself with gentleness, humor, love, and respect.

AUTOPOESIS AND GUIDANCE THE INNER HEALER ARCHETYPE

One of the principles of the cosmos is that all life has the ability to manifest itself, and this is referred to as autopoesis. Autopoesis holds that there is an inner capacity within all of life, within the cells of our body, within the soil, stars, trees, and all things to participate directly in the endeavor of creation.[3] It is the capacity for self-manifestation. Within every eye cell, for example, is the knowledge of how to be an eye. Within skin cells is the ability to engage in the process of healing a wound. This principle tells us that as members of creation, we have the inherent ability to heal ourselves and to evolve and become who we really are. Through imagery, we concretize this awareness and we align with its energy.

Another way to understand this is to look at the process of trauma and healing vortices. Within the energy of a trauma is the resource (the healing vortex) needed to balance the nervous system.[4] Similarly, within each life experience is the ability to deal with it. That ability is stored in the body along with the trauma itself. This ability is not always conscious. It speaks to the body's knowledge of how to heal itself and reminds us that the subconscious mind is not *in* the body but *is the body itself.*[5] Therefore, accessing the body through the language of sensation and imagery can impact our healing. In this way, we increase our resources and our ability to meet life.

When we are hurt, we tend to feel isolated and alienated. To bridge this gap, in *The Spiral of Healing,* we follow a guided visualization to meet this energy and then we image that guide. By doing this, we use our imagination to bring the autopoetic principle into conscious awareness, and we deepen the new relationship we are building with our body, spirit, and mind.

Please continue on in this chapter and begin the creative processes. If you need to review preparation for them, see Section Three, "How to Use This Book." You can follow along if you have the accompanying CD.

CREATIVE PROCESSES

I. BEGINNING SELF-PORTRAIT

This process creates a baseline or a beginning image to the start of the journey and gives you important information about yourself. Use the questions in the writing section to connect more deeply with your image and perhaps discover some of the themes you will be learning about.

MATERIALS

Meditative instrumental music
The Spiral of Healing CD
Art materials
Journal or other writing notebook and pen

MOVEMENT

Turn on the music and begin by moving to its rhythms. Allow yourself to feel your energy move as you sway, and gently begin to move your body. Bring your awareness to your feet, ankles, shins, and knees, and move up your body until you have slowly moved every part of it that you can, including your jaw and eyes. Spend up to about five minutes with this.

Find your center by going off balance: rest your weight on one foot and then the other, tip forward and back, and gently rock back and forth and side to side until you sense an inner point of balance. Take a few minutes to do this.

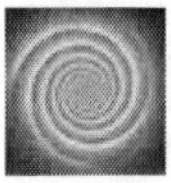

GUIDED VISUALIZATION

Turn off the music and stand, lie down, or sit quietly. Check in with yourself. Sense what is moving through you, where you feel tight or loose, tired or energized. Ask yourself: What does my life feel like right now? How do I see myself? How do I feel about myself? You don't have to know all of the answers. In fact, meditate on the questions themselves until you have a general impression. It will clarify as you continue. When you are ready, go on to the art process.

ART PROCESS: BEGINNING SELF-PORTRAIT

As with all of the art processes in this book, focus on your process not the product. To warm up, you may like to do some preliminary scribbles with oil pastels or crayons. These are random motions on the paper. Try doing one with eyes open, another with eyes closed, and one with the left and then the right hands. Do one with both hands, eyes open and closed. Drawing this freely can help loosen up your self-judgment. Remember, what you create is for your eyes only and will inform you well about your present state. There is no right way, only *your* way.

Using whatever materials seem most descriptive of how you feel right now, create an image of yourself. Your self-portrait can be abstract or realistic and can include physical, emotional, mental, and spiritual aspects. Allow as much time as you need for this.

WRITING

Try dialoguing with the image on paper, in your journal or on separate large sheets of blank paper. To do this, you'll communicate with the image itself, as if it has come to talk with you and give you the gift of teaching you more about yourself. Using your dominant hand (if you are right-handed, this would be your right hand), welcome the image and ask it why it has come or what it is about (even if you think you know). You'll "hear" the answers in your imagination as you write them with your non-dominant hand. They may come in incomplete sentences and may not even make sense. Just keep with the process until there is some resolution or you wish to stop. Remember that imagery is a gift from your unconscious self and can open up doorways into building a healthy relationship between your mind and your body. If you like, read the dialogue aloud and write it into your journal if you have not already done that.

Next, ask yourself these questions, and write your answers:

1. What do I see when I look at this image? (Act as if you have never seen it before—see lines, colors, movement. Try not to jump to interpretation.)
2. What is missing from this image?
3. What does it tell me about myself?
4. How do I feel about this image?
5. What would I change if I could?

II. FINDING A SAFE PLACE IN YOUR BODY

This process gives you an embodied anchor of safety, nourishment, beauty, and calmness and can create a new neurological pathway in your brain and the beginning of a new relationship with your own body. Use it as a daily meditation, and you will begin to sense these qualities in a real way within you. In times of stress, you will find it available as a way to sooth yourself.

MATERIALS

Meditative instrumental music
The Spiral of Healing CD
Art materials
Journal or other writing notebook and pen

MOVEMENT

WAKING UP THE BODY

This movement process will be used many times throughout the book. Refer to this page as needed or record it onto a tape to use as a guide. You can also order *The Spiral of Healing* CD (see Audio Resources). Be sure to pause three to five seconds wherever " . . ." is indicated.

Stand comfortably, allowing yourself plenty of room for movement. If you cannot stand, sit in such a way as to allow for as much movement as possible. This is an opportunity for you to make contact with your body.

Begin by breathing normally and maintain awareness of your breath. Starting with your toes, wiggle and wake them up . . . If you have pain anywhere, pay attention to it, rub it, and be kind to yourself . . . Rotate your ankles and toes, feel the balls of your feet, and imagine the energy rising, entering into your feet with your breath . . . Slowly travel up your calves to your knees, the place of flexibility, and then into your thigh area . . . Follow the music, moving around in place, exploring awareness of all of the parts of your feet and legs. There is no right or wrong way to do anything on this tape, just your way . . .

Now, move through the hip area, rocking your hips from side to side, front to back . . . Try a "figure eight" pattern, loosening, relaxing, moving, and waking up your body . . . Make contact with your lower back, the base of your spine, by rubbing it . . . Say hello to your waist and your belly, these wonderful parts of us . . . Move up into the solar plexus area, under the ribs, where all those inner organs work without thought . . . The liver, gall bladder, stomach, intestines do their work quietly. Touch your body, move it around so that you become aware of the midback and solar plexus area.

Next, move up into the chest area, into the heart space. Stretch your arms, feeling their length. See if you can open up this part of your body . . . Travel to the high part of your back and shoulders and work them forward and backward, up and down, loosening as you move . . . Travel down your arms, using your hands to rub your shoulders, your upper arms down to your elbows, your forearms down to your wrists, and into the palms of your hands and your fingers. Let your fingers do their own dance, moving, opening . . . Think of all these wonderful parts of our body do for us, how grateful we are for them . . .

Come back up into the neck area, the place that helps us breathe, helps us speak, and open your mouth . . . Rub the back of your neck and jaw, loosening your jaw. Massage your ears, open them up, and see if you can feel warmth spreading through your body . . . Travel up into your sinus areas—your nose, eyes—gently rub them, massaging the sockets and brow area . . . Wake up the scalp and other parts of your head by gently scratching, rubbing, visualizing your head breathing, waking up . . .

Scan from the top of your head down to your toes . . . Let your awareness drift as the day's events wash off of you and away . . . as if you are standing under a waterfall. If there is any place in particular that is calling your attention, a part of your body that hurts or feels a little tweaked, rub it some more and notice what feels open and what feels tense and closed . . .

For a few moments, let yourself be entirely present, here, in your body . . . Welcome your body to join you on this journey so that you can receive the gifts that your imagination and your body want to give you.

When you are ready, find a comfortable place to sit, recline, or stand, and continue the journey with the next part of the process.

GUIDED VISUALIZATION

This exercise is designed to begin the process of building an awareness of sensations, thoughts, feelings and images into a more concrete form. There is never a right or wrong way to do this, only your way. And whatever happens to you on this journey, whether you follow the directions or find yourself doing a variation on them, accept it as the gift that it is. In doing this short meditation daily, you will create a new neurological pathway that can be available to you during times of high stress.

Let your attention wander to a part of your body that feels neutral to good and which has no discomfort or pain. It can be a part as small as the tip of your finger. The only requirement is that it is a part of your body that is completely free from discomfort or tension.

If you happen to have a lot of physical pain, find an area that is the least difficult for you.

I invite you now to give your attention to this part. Imagine that within this part, there is a doorway, or portal, leading inside . . . Look at this doorway, gateway, or other opening. Notice the color; notice the texture . . . I invite you to move through this doorway . . . and as you do, find yourself in a place on the other side of it. What is here? Take notice. It can be a real or an imaginary place. It doesn't have to conform to nature at all . . .

It is a very special place, a *safe* place . . . The most incredible thing about this place is that you have absolute control of it. This place is full of wondrous goodies, energies, and qualities—for you. Invite these qualities in, bring them in, notice how these qualities make you feel . . . Nothing enters; nothing leaves without your desire. Even getting to this place—you are the only one who knows how to do that . . . That in itself makes it safe . . .

In this place, you can feel safe like you have never felt before . . . Not only do you have total control—nothing and no one can enter unless you want them to—but this is also a place where you are safe from your own negative thoughts, judgments, and critiques . . .

Look around; call in what makes you feel safe. Surround yourself with the feeling of safety. What brings you the feeling, the wonder, the body sensation of "here I am truly safe" . . . Notice color . . . texture . . . lightness . . . heaviness . . . Notice any smell . . . and any sound . . .

Using your imagination, create this container, this place for yourself where you can finally be . . . (Allow one minute in silence.)

Besides safety, another quality that lives in this place is *nourishment*. This is a place where you are fed on every level—mentally . . . physically . . . emotionally . . . spiritually . . . sexually . . . in this place you are nourished . . . Look around. Call in all those favorite ways that you can feel nourished in your life . . . Colors and textures, shapes, beings, whatever you need . . . Give yourself permission to have this, to give this to yourself . . . (Allow one minute in silence.)

As you meander through this place, feeling fed on so many levels and feeling safe . . . I'd like you to notice that in this place, you feel serene and calm . . . there is no need to strive in this place . . . You have already arrived . . . This is the place where all of you is accepted and acceptable . . . and you can relax in deep, deep serenity and be rested . . . You can rest into a sense of deep, deep calmness and serenity . . . All of your senses come alive in this place . . . Let the sounds and the smells nourish you, bringing you what you need . . . (Allow one minute in silence.)

Another quality that lives in this place is *nurturance . . .* When you are here, you feel held . . . you feel seen . . . and you feel heard . . . You get what you need without even asking for it . . . This amazing place is all yours . . . You can be nurtured, uplifted, deeply cared for in this place . . . Let your heart open to it . . . Let yourself drink this in . . . and whatever colors and images that come to you. Remember, you have control over this place . . . You can bring in anything and everything here that supports your feeling safe and serene, nourished, and nurtured . . . (Allow one minute in silence.)

The final quality that lives in this place is the quality of *pleasure and beauty . . .* There is incredible pleasure in everything you feel . . . touch . . . smell . . . and see . . . in everything you taste . . . everything you hear . . . Notice what is you would love to have that would bring you this quality, and invite it in now . . . bring it into this wondrous place inside of you. And again, feel that pleasure on all levels—physically . . . sexually . . . mentally . . . emotionally . . . spiritually.

As you meander through this place, letting yourself open up to these qualities that are here for you, remember this is yours and you can have this experience anytime that you want . . . It is connected to you, to the doorway, to your body . . . It lives and breathes inside of you . . . You can come here whenever you like . . . If you have time in your day to luxuriate in this place, do it as much as you can. If you don't, let yourself anchor it to something you do regularly, like showering. When you shower, then you go through your doorway and find yourself in this place of rest and renewal, regeneration . . . You can feel these qualities growing in you . . . This is a work in progress; it grows and changes as you deepen the experience.

I am going to invite you now to step back through the doorway. Take a last look around for now . . . and when you feel ready, wiggle your toes, feel your feet on the ground, feel your body on the chair or wherever you are . . . Gently wake up, remembering your connection to this place, remembering where you are.

Keep this feeling alive and flowing as you go to the art materials and recreate it in some way.

ART PROCESS: FINDING A SAFE PLACE IN YOUR BODY

Create an image of your embodied safe place that expresses the feeling of it as well as the look. It may be abstract or literal. Senses may be represented—sights, sounds, tastes, smells, textures—and any other sensations. Remember, this is a work in progress; it doesn't have to be finished in one sitting. You can change or add to it as you continue to experience this inner realm.

When you're done, title the image, put it where you can see it before you go to bed at night or when you wake in the morning to remind you of your safe, nourishing place. Spend time in your safe place. Take yourself to your safe place to be rejuvenated at least once a day for a few minutes until you feel some of the qualities that live there. Allow yourself to create a new option when you feel activated or stressed.

WRITING

Journal your experience.

III. CREATING A SHIELD OF PROTECTION

Using your imagination to create a powerful symbol of protection and boundary allows you to experience the energy within. It also allows your adult self to reclaim the job of protection.

MATERIALS

Art materials, including firm cardboard
The Spiral of Healing CD
Journal or other writing notebook and pen

MOVEMENT

BOUNDARIES: PART I

This exercise involves a partner. Begin by standing comfortably with plenty of room around you. Sense yourself in your body as you reach as far as you can above, below, in front, and at the back of you. The edge of your personal space is the farthest you can reach while standing. Get used to sensing yourself filling this space. Notice the directions in which you may have difficulty filling the space. Practice expanding your energy to fill it.

Turn to your partner, and stand facing each other, about eight feet apart. That person will remain stationary and be in charge of and paying attention to his or herself. When he or she is ready, he or she will begin to slowly walk toward you. As he or she does, sense where you feel connected to this person but not intruded upon. This is your comfort zone. When the person reaches it, ask him or her to stop. Now, measure with your arm how far away the person is. This usually corresponds to the edge of your personal space. It can differ quite a bit according to differences in gender, age, and height.

Let your partner walk up very close to you so you can sense what that feels like. Next, ask him or her to step back slowly until you are comfortable again. When you are, ask him or her to stop. For those with little sense of boundaries or those doing this exercise with a person already close to you, the distance will be much smaller. Notice again where in your body you feel both the discomfort and comfort of someone near or within your energy field.

Repeat this movement with your eyes closed. Your partner will say, "I am stepping closer," over and over as they do so. When he or she is as close to you as you feel comfortable letting him or her be, ask him or her to stop. He or she will then begin to step back from you. When he or she has retreated to your point of comfort, let him or her know. Notice how you feel with your eyes closed and with your eyes open.

Repeat this movement now with your back to your partner. Do it first with your eyes open and then with them closed. Again, notice how you feel with someone walking up close to your back.

Switch roles, allowing your partner to be stationary while you are the walker. When you have finished all four movements, share your experiences with each other. Discuss what you noticed about yourself.

During the rest of the day, as you walk around, notice how easily you enter other people's space. Be aware of how you let others into your space. Begin to sense what your body does in reaction to others entering your private space.

BOUNDARIES: PART II

In a group or with another person, practice owning your space. Take a long piece of yarn or string and create a circle on the ground large enough to include all of your personal space. Step into the center of it and feel its boundaries. Ask others to stand outside that circle. Maintaining eye contact, one by one, say to them, "This is my personal space and you may not enter without my permission." Allow for plenty of time to absorb and process your feelings as you do this. You can use any tone you need to in order to sense you are speaking your truth and that you mean it.

Take your place outside the circle and let the next person do the exercise. Experience how it feels to be told this and receive it. Notice where in your body you have a reaction or response to both declaring a boundary and/or receiving someone else's declaration.

GUIDED VISUALIZATION

Scan your body for a place of vulnerability . . . Notice where you would like to feel more protected . . . Choose one part and focus on it, noticing any sensations present as you acknowledge your vulnerability . . .

Imagine what you would need to feel safe and protected in this area . . . Imagine a form of protection . . . a structure . . . a person or group of people . . . an animal . . . an element . . . a texture . . . or color . . . that would soothe and allow you to relax and soften this part of yourself . . . Give yourself permission to invite any of this and all that you need to create a protective shield for you . . . Invite your inner Warrior archetype to be present . . . You might imagine this Warrior in any form you like; its job is to protect and defend you in a way that is helpful for you.

ART PROCESS: CREATING A SHIELD OF PROTECTION

When you feel you have connected with a protective energy in some form, use a piece of cardboard and create the shape of your shield, decorating it with images, colors, textures—whatever it is that represents what you have experienced inside yourself. Title the image.

WRITING

Work with the energies of the shield. Practice holding the completed shield in front of your vulnerable area and breathe in the protection. Sense protection in your body. Notice where you feel vulnerable and imagine the shield bringing you comfort and protection. Notice what changes in your body. Write your experiences in your journal.

IV. FINDING YOUR INNER HEALER GUIDE

Guidance can take many forms. It can come in the form of archetypal energies. It can be an awareness of faith or a sense of longing to know something greater than ourselves.

The Inner Healer Guide is a symbol of the imaginal experience aligning with the physical. The Inner Healer Guide also begins our connection to guidance, which is the experience we have when we no longer feel alone. Connection to spirit gives us the sense that we have a purpose for living and an essential place here.

We use the imaginal process to travel to the "over-world," which connects us to ancestors, spirits, and wisdom. In the same way, we travel to the "underworld" of mystery, shadow, and the unknown, where we find and retrieve lost energies and the jewels of our healing. When we've journeyed in these realms, we bring our new awareness back to the middle world of our everyday experience of functioning, and we practice these new behaviors and strategies with a feeling of support and strength.

Make daily contact with your Inner Healer Guide. Sense your guide's presence in your body. Build a relationship with this energy.

MATERIALS

Art materials, including firm cardboard
The Spiral of Healing CD
Journal or other writing notebook and pen

MOVEMENT

Begin with the "Waking Up the Body" exercise. When you finish, give yourself time to scan your body and comfort any aches or tensions you may feel. Then lie down or sit comfortably, and allow yourself to relax and focus inward.

GUIDED VISUALIZATION

As with "Finding a Safe Place in Your Body," allow yourself to focus on a body part that feels good to neutral . . . and see the doorway or portal to it. Allow yourself to go through that doorway, and find yourself in your safe place again . . .

This time you also notice a path. As you gently walk the path, notice colors, textures, sounds, and smells that accompany you on your walk . . . Notice the temperature and your own inner excitement growing . . . You are walking this path to meet someone who has wanted to meet you for a long time . . . This energy has been with you always and has wanted to work consciously with you for some time . . .

As you continue walking, notice a being or energy approaching you. Joy fills your heart . . . Soon, you will be very close, so begin to notice the details of what is before you . . . What is the particular form, if there is one? If it is more elusive than formed, simply feel the energy surrounding you . . . You are meeting a very important guide who is here to accompany you on your healing journey . . . This guide knows the way. Its entire purpose for being is to support your process.

Begin to communicate with this guide in whatever way is possible . . . Ask a question . . . Listen to the answer . . . Spend a few minutes with your Inner Healer Guide. If the guide has a name, find out what it is so you can call on your guide with that name . . . As you converse, allow yourself to receive answers in multiple sensorial ways . . . Notice your body and your sensations as you imagine this conversation of sorts . . . If the guide has a task for you, ask what that is . . . If the guide has a gift, receive it . . . Allow some time for silence. See what happens inside of it.

Say goodbye for now to your guide and begin to return along the path to the doorway . . . Go through the doorway and come back into the room . . . Wiggle your fingers and toes, and gently open your eyes.

ART PROCESS: FINDING YOUR INNER HEALER GUIDE

When you are fully present, take your art materials and create an image of your Inner Healer Guide. Allow yourself to create something three-dimensional if you have not done so before. Try some new art materials, and remember to play and get messy. Give yourself plenty of time to capture your experience. Title your image.

WRITING

Journal about the guided visualization and your art piece. Dialogue with it as you did internally with your guide, and see if you can learn any more about your healing process.

ADDITIONAL EXERCISES

1. This month, spend at least fifteen minutes daily alone and in silence. Experience how you feel when you are aware of your boundaries.
2. s you review the list of signs of healthy boundaries, discover how many are true for you. Which do you have difficulty with? Make a commitment to strengthening your boundaries by incorporating these signs.
3. Practice the boundary exercises in this chapter with a different person or group. Feel your personal space in different situations and with different types of people (children, men, women, tall and short, strangers and intimates). Pay attention to your body as you do these exercises.
4. Work with the energies of the shield. Sense protection in your body. Notice where you feel vulnerable and imagine the shield bringing you comfort and protection. Notice what changes in your body.

5. Make daily contact with your Inner Healer Guide. Sense your guide's presence in your body. Build a relationship with this energy.
6. Spend time in your safe place. Allow yourself to create a new option when you feel activated or stressed. Take yourself to your safe place to be rejuvenated at least once a day for a few minutes until you feel some of the qualities that live there.

QUESTIONS TO PONDER

1. Under what circumstances do you allow others into your personal space?
2. Who do you let cross your boundaries and why? With whom do you have difficulty speaking your truth? In what areas of your life do you speak up for yourself and others? Do you honor and respect the limits and boundaries of others as well as yourself? In what ways do boundaries both challenge and inspire you?
3. With whom or in what situations have you felt oppressed?
4. How do you protect yourself? What strategies have you used and how successful are they?
5. What is your relationship to guidance? How do you experience your connection to wisdom and support? Is that support internal as well as external? How do you sense guidance in your body?
6. How do you sense safety in your life? To what do you attribute your feelings of safety or lack of it?
7. What feeds you emotionally, spiritually, mentally, and physically?
8. How have you or do you currently feel contented and in deep rest? How do you sense this in your body?
9. Do you feel held in your life? Do you have a sense of being seen and heard and that your needs are important and cared for? In what ways?
10. Where do you experience pleasure in your life? In what ways would you like to increase this feeling?
11. What is your relationship to your body? Do you like it? How do you feel in your body? What would you change about it if you could?
12. How do you feel about your mind? What thoughts bother you? How do you use your mind in your daily life?

13. What is your relationship to your emotions? Can you access the full range of emotions, and if not, which ones are difficult for you? What goals would you choose for yourself emotionally?
14. What is your spiritual experience? Do you feel connected to something larger than your personal story? If so, what and how do you practice staying in touch with it? How important is spirituality to you?
15. What is your relationship to creativity? How do you define being creative? What would you change about your experience of creativity?

PART II

JOURNEY THROUGH THE CHAKRAS

1.

LAYING THE FOUNDATION

RETRIEVING THE HEALTHY CHILD
Root (First) Chakra

A smart person takes play seriously,
For in the act of playing
Is the possibility of going beyond established borders.
—Matthew Fox

As young children, we need safety and permission to explore. We need touch and attention to our needs, which at first seem purely physical. We cry when we are wet, hungry, tired, or in need of touch. If we receive what we need, we are content and get on with the business of exploring our bodies and the world around us. If we do not receive what we need, we spend a great deal of time trying to deal with anxious, uncomfortable, and confusing sensations. If we get overwhelmed, our nervous systems will shut down to compensate, as we do not have access to our emotions or thoughts and must rely on others to make sense of our experience. Therefore, our original tribal or family experiences are crucial and foundational. We need to feel safe and connected and to know we belong. We are instinctual beings, and when we sense safety and connectedness in our bodies, we grow and develop in health. If our early life experiences are supportive, we assimilate information easily and we internalize healthy, effective modeling.

THE IMPACT OF YOUR FAMILY COMMUNITY

The purpose of tribal communities is continuation of the tribe. We learn about such values as loyalty, honor, trust, and honesty, which serve to keep the collective functioning. We also learn about justice, tolerance, and sexuality. The individual is not the concern of the tribe and is often sacrificed for the homeostasis of the community. Love is generally expressed as physical—food, clothing, and shelter—and not as building self-esteem, supporting the needs of the individual, or appreciating diversity, unless this is seen as supporting the collective. Since the child needs these qualities to be healthy, the family dynamic can and will be at cross-purposes with the individual.

As a small child, our primary needs are for belonging, safety, and survival, and these supersede our desire to be seen and loved for our uniqueness. If necessary, we relegate those secondary needs to the background and follow the tribal influence, which works if the family system is encouraging and supportive and we agree with its values. If we encounter toxic tribal energies, however, in the form of abuse, neglect, rigidity, overprotection, or disconnection, we lack proper guidance and instruction and do not receive the mirroring we need to develop healthy traits. We then struggle with an ability to provide for ourselves, to stand up for ourselves, to know what we want and how to get it, or to be able to trust in a larger context and receive guidance.

As there is no separation between body, mind, and spirit, we receive and store all experience in our physical body. If our early experiences are toxic, we sense those energies in our body; our body speaks to us in a language of sensation. Toxic experiences may be communicated as physical pain or constriction. Over time, we may develop physical symptoms that refer back to early emotional, spiritual, or developmental trauma.

Systemic body processes and physical body support fall under the domain of the first chakra. This knowledge can point us in the right direction for healing. By understanding how our nervous system responded to experiences in our childhood, we can learn ways of releasing uncomfortable sensations from our body. Awareness is always the first step.

ARCHETYPAL ENERGIES OF THE FIRST CHAKRA

If tribal influences are the foundation of the root chakra, then the energy of the child is its primary archetypal structure. We often think of childhood as a blessed time, but for some, it is an experience of the shattering of innocence. The hurt, neglect, or abuse that many feel when they are young can awaken a deep sense of purpose (to heal and help others) and/or become the lens through which lifelong learning happens. What seems clear is that from the experience of early pain, the hurt child or victim archetype is born.

As an innocent child, we are happy, trusting, and playful. As a wounded child, we are angry, fearful, and painfully aware of our needs being unmet. Depending on our experience, we form survival strategies, among which are the archetypes of the Saboteur and the Prostitute.[1] The Saboteur's strategy is to control bad things by making them happen. In this way, we feel some sense of control over our lives, though we may carry a core belief that only bad things can happen. The Prostitute's strategy is to give up aspects of ourselves in order to be safe, loved, or supported. It operates on the belief that we must give up who we are in order to get what we need.

We can also look at the wounded child through four distinct aspects or coping mechanisms.[2] These are creative strategies that develop after one is hurt and is trying to respond through behavior. If left unchecked these coping mechanisms become the shadow side of the archetypes of the healthy Warrior, Healer, Visionary, and Teacher in adult life.

1. The adult shadow Warrior is the rebel. A childhood strategy is the brat or tyrant. The tyrant is the child who has too much power in the family because the parents lack authority or are unwilling to be firm and loving in their discipline.
2. The adult shadow Healer is the victim/martyr. A childhood strategy is the pouting, silent, withdrawn child. This child feels powerless and gains some control by going mute or isolating.
3. The adult shadow Visionary or Strategist is the manipulator or controller. A childhood strategy is the deceptive, clever, and sly child. He or she tries to get needs met by lying or withholding.
4. The adult shadow Teacher is the judgmental moralist or critic. A childhood strategy is the precocious, righteous, know-it-all, indignant child. This child feels unworthy but tries to make up for it by performing.

To heal these parts of ourselves, we must become aware of and then embrace the qualities of each archetype creatively and then transform the shadow energies within us.[3] In the work of the root chakra, we will begin to unlock some of these truths and start the process of healing.

A strong sense of self requires a balance of active Child and Adult archetypes. The archetypal energies of the Innocent and the Orphan and the adult archetypal energies of the Warrior and the Caregiver are a good example. The Innocent establishes our persona, or the masks we wear, in the world. It is a social role whose goal is safety and love. The Innocent carries a belief that she will be cared for in the world. The Innocent's fear is of abandonment. The shadow side of that is denial, naiveté, and blame of others. Once the Innocent has been hurt, the Orphan blossoms. The positive Orphan recognizes the limits of the world, figures out how to take care of herself, and bands together with other Orphans for creating support. The negative Orphan experiences cynicism, disillusionment, and betrayal and carries the core belief that no one can help her. With a mature Caregiver who loves and teaches and a strong Warrior who protects, the Child energies come into balance and support each other.[4] We can be all of these for ourselves.

RETRIEVING THE HEALTHY CHILD THROUGH THE CREATIVE ARTS

The creative process supports the awakening of the energies of the first chakra in many ways. Art-making and playfulness fall into the realm of the child, and by allowing ourselves playtime in the creative arts, we encourage a healthy relationship with our adult and child selves. We give permission for the child in us to make messes, to take risks, to develop skill, and to grow a healthy self-esteem. That is why it feels so good to be creative. When we are not creating images to be "artistically correct," we can relax and allow an innocent, curious, and explorative part of ourselves to emerge. Being creative also connects us to our own divinity and our ability to bring forth something from nothing. Whether we create from awe and blessing or from darkness and pain, we transform our experience through the act of making art.

Because all memory is stored in the body as sensation and imagery, we can use the creative arts to retrieve and transform thoughts and emotions that surround traumatic events. We do this by connecting with our sensations and putting color, texture, and image to them. Making art allows us to move gently into an altered state of consciousness and encourages the trauma state–dependent imagery to emerge. Once we have an image, we can dialogue with it to learn what we need to do to help it transform. It is our active participation in the creative healing process that contributes to our emotional and physical resolution of trauma.

ALL IS ONE

By engaging our creativity with our body, mind, and spirit, we experience the sacred truth of the root chakra, or "All is One."[5] Knowing this truth allows us to experience that we are connected to all life and that every choice we make and every belief we hold exerts influence on the larger community within ourselves, with each other, with the Earth, and with all creation. We experience unity out of separation, wholeness out of fragmentation, and trust out of victimization.

Awareness of our unity and the illusion of separation are first learned in our original community and set the stage for our learning path. By waking up to the truth of our interrelatedness with all life, we can overcome many obstacles and make sense of our histories. We can come into the present moment and connect with our life purpose while feeling the support of the universe. When we do, trust becomes the foundation and compassion the path.

CREATIVE PROCESSES

I. SENSING YOUR FIRST CHAKRA ENERGY

This process takes you into the root chakra of your body in a new way through sensing, imaging, and feeling. It will help you uncover early childhood experiences.

MATERIALS

Meditative instrumental music
The Spiral of Healing CD
Simple art materials a child could use such as paper, clay, finger paint (no scissors or rulers)
Journal or other writing notebook and pen

MOVEMENT

Begin with "Waking Up the Body" (page 59, or use CD).

GUIDED VISUALIZATION

Scan your body, and pay attention to how it is speaking to you through sensations.

Recall yourself as a child under the age of seven . . . What are you doing? What are you playing? Where are you? See yourself in a scene, noticing colors, textures, sounds, smells, temperature . . . Notice your relationship to nature, to animals, to the physical world . . . Are you biking or skating, playing in the dirt, or playing with dolls, balls, or other toys? Are you climbing? Notice how you feel remembering yourself this young . . . Notice your legs and arms and how much you used them as a child.

How do you feel doing those activities today? What is different from how you felt doing them as a young child?

ART PROCESS: SENSING YOUR FIRST CHAKRA ENERGY

Using your non-dominant hand, scribble, tear paper, play with clay, get messy, and don't think too much. Use no straight edges. Notice how your body feels when you play. Have fun and create.

When you are finished, title your art piece.

WRITING

Journal about your experience.

II. CREATING YOUR LITTLE ONE

Creating a doll of a part of your child archetype that you may not be so familiar with is another way to connect with and relate to a lost or hidden aspect of your childhood experience.

MATERIALS

Meditative instrumental music
The Spiral of Healing CD
Muslin doll forms (see Art Materials Resources, page 223)
Fabric of various colors and/or textures
Hot glue gun and glue
Sewing materials
Paints and brushes
Beads, buttons, bows, yarn, stickers—decorations of any type
Journal or other writing book and pen

MOVEMENT

Begin with "Waking Up the Body" (see page 59, or use CD).

GUIDED VISUALIZATION

Get into a comfortable position—whether standing, lying down, or sitting—and allow yourself to connect with your feelings and thoughts about your childhood. Notice which aspects of your child self seem familiar and which feel foreign. When you think about balancing the wounded child with the healthy or divine child, what might be missing for you? If you play the innocent child a lot and haven't really allowed yourself to be angry or wild, imagine that part of you coming alive. Feel it in your body. Allow yourself to move in ways that would give pleasure to that child aspect you rarely allow to come forward. If you tend to be serious, call in the silly, funny, playful child. Let yourself to move in ways that support this new aspect. What would this child wear? What colors would express this part of the child?

ART PROCESS: CREATING YOUR LITTLE ONE

When you have an idea of who you would like to bring forward, take the muslin doll form and create the image of what you would like to have more of in your life.

WRITING

Journal about your experience.

III. TORN-PAPER COLLAGE

This process brings you into a further awareness both spatially and creatively with the way you felt in relationship physically and emotionally with your family members. Pay attention to the questions in the writing section as they will deepen your experience of this image.

MATERIALS
Large sheet of white paper
The Spiral of Healing CD
Smaller assorted colors of construction paper
Glue
Journal or other writing notebook and pen
Scissors are discouraged.

MOVEMENT

Begin by turning on the music and gently moving, waking up your awareness of yourself in your body. (Use CD for "Waking Up the Body," or see page 59.)

GUIDED VISUALIZATION

Remember yourself at an age before seven years . . . Who were the significant people in your world? You can choose a difficult or easy time, and you can include anyone of significance, even those outside your immediate family.

ART PROCESS: TORN PAPER COLLAGE

As with all of the art processes, allow yourself to let go of the results and focus on how you feel as you do the process.

Take the construction paper, and tear it to create yourself and those in your life at that time. You can use color and shape to distinguish each of the significant people. Glue these forms onto the white paper. When you are finished, title the piece.

WRITING

What do you notice about the images on the paper? How do the images feel to you? Is there anything you would you change? Where are you in relation to your parents, if they are here? Who is the largest/smallest one on the paper? Who is touching another? What do you sense in your body as you notice the placement of these images on the paper? Write about your reflections.

ADDITIONAL EXERCISES

1. Honor your body by making a daily connection with it. Touch each part and thank it for its hard work (*Thank you, feet, for taking me where I need to go. Thank you, knees, for allowing me to be flexible*). Start with the area of the first chakra, and after reading each chapter, add the next chakra when you practice this body honoring.
2. Spend a few moments each day making contact with the little one within you. Either write or internally dialog with whatever aspect that wants to talk with you. Ask what is needed, and acknowledge all feelings without trying to fix anything. What beliefs did you inherit from your family or community? Which of those still affect you although they may no longer be valid?
3. What are some of the blessings and challenges you received from your family?
4. In what situations or with what people do you feel trust? How do you sense this in your body?
5. What behavioral and emotional strategies did you form as a child in order to live in your family? Which ones do you still use, and are they effective?
6. Of the four shadow Child archetypes, which, if any, are still active? How do they manifest in your adult life?
7. To which aspects of your life do you bring curiosity and playfulness? In what areas do you deny these childlike qualities?

2.

Entering the Fruitful Dark

Finding Your Way with Creativity, Sexuality, and Work
Sacral (Second) Chakra

To bring light into the dark
is to know the light.
To know the dark,
go dark, go without sight.
And find that the darkness blooms and sings.
And is traveled
by dark feet and dark wings.
—*Wendell Berry*

While the process of first chakra development is centered on group identity and learning, the second chakra energizes us to develop our sense of power in the external world through relationships, sexuality, creativity, money, and work. From the sensation of oneness or symbiosis (with mother and group), we now begin to experience a duality of energy, male/female, yin/yang, and we learn to dance with the opposites. Here, a child feels her separation and tackles the issues of "what's mine and what's yours." We also experience sexuality and emotions, the power of choice and control. We reclaim the right to feel and the sacred truth to honor one another. The spiritual challenge of the second chakra is to learn to interact consciously with others, to draw people who support our development to us, and to release relationships that handicap our growth.

Experiencing second chakra energy requires a letting go of intellect. We swim in an ocean of feelings and sensations without much thought. In this way, we enter the "fruitful dark." This part of our being is multilayered; we gather and sort information in a sea of complexity. Physically, we are working with the ability to create and generate life while we work with the elimination of physical matter that no longer serves us. Emotionally, we strive for balance between a sense of belonging and a move toward autonomy. Spiritually, we learn to receive, create, and let go.

Emotions are energy in motion. When we receive sensory input, our body translates our cellular response into feelings. These feelings move through us and guide our responses. When we experience the attraction of opposites, we invite movement or the instinctual pull to expand ourselves by sensing something different. We learn how to stay connected to ourselves in relationships and other situations, how to take risks, and to develop will. Where we were controlled by the group identity, we now seek to find our own ways of controlling the dynamics of our physical environment. We use our will to establish our authority, to overcome our fear of losing control or being controlled by others. We learn to handle our physical needs and make choices that work for us. We strive to develop intimate relationships that support our learning.

Using our creativity for our survival, we discover how to take the values received from our community and support ourselves. We make our beliefs and goals public through the work we do. We begin to utilize the values of our tribe, especially the issues of integrity, honesty, and trust, and we are attracted to work that supports them. In order to accomplish all this, we must be connected to our feelings, our creativity, our sexual energy, and our power. We begin to explore all of these in the second chakra.

EARLY DEVELOPMENT AND THE SECOND CHAKRA

The task of the young child is to grow while staying connected, to explore her boundaries in a safe and controlled environment. If she is allowed security and safety, noninvasive touch, and pleasant stimulation, she will begin to expand her area of exploration and test the waters as she moves farther away from her mother. From symbiosis, she journeys to autonomy.

During her second year, the young child begins the process of what is called "rapprochement." Rapprochement means the establishment of cordial relationships, or reciprocity. This is a significant aspect of human development based on having a good sense of parental attachment and proceeding to the establishment of autonomy and sense of self.

To better understand rapprochement, let us look at a young child playing in the sandbox at the park. Mom is sitting nearby talking to another mom. At first, the young child plays independently from Mom. She soon realizes that she is alone and turns to find her mother. The mother's response to her determines whether or not this young child continues in her movement to autonomy in a secure way. If the child looks back to see a relaxed, smiling mother, the child knows she is okay to proceed to play alone. If she looks back and sees a fearful mother being overprotective and controlling, she will stay where she is but may feel confused, anxious, or fearful about her continued play.

If she looks back to find her mother ignoring her, she will run over to get her attention. If the attention is positive when she gets there, she will restart the process of rapprochement. If the attention is negative, she will stay close, often clinging to her mother until she gets the attention she needs. If she is neglected or rejected, she will return to her play with her needs unmet.

If this happens frequently, she will make decisions about her needs and most likely begin to repress them to avoid pain. Her need is to belong. Rejected, she will begin to view all basic needs as wrong and she will disconnect from herself when she feels needy. Over time, this child will grow into an adult woman and develop a self-image that prohibits needs; and she will become anxious or withdrawn when others need her. Or, from her early experience of abandonment or isolation, she will develop a strategy of taking care of others as the only way to satisfy her need to belong. Either way, she loses her connection to herself; and as she grows, she will have difficulty caring for her needs. She will tend to attract people who reinforce her negative self-concept, and she will likely perpetuate the cycle with her own children.

To transform this early conditioning and the patterns in her mother line, the grown woman must reclaim the right to her feelings and her needs. By creating safety for herself by listening to her intuition and taking risks to ask for what she needs, she can complete her early developmental process and achieve a sense of wholeness for herself. From here, she can connect with a healthy adult partner and find her sovereignty within an interdependent relationship.

The following diagram shows one example of the development and individuation path in healthy relationships.

Figure 4
Individuation Diagram
In Relationships

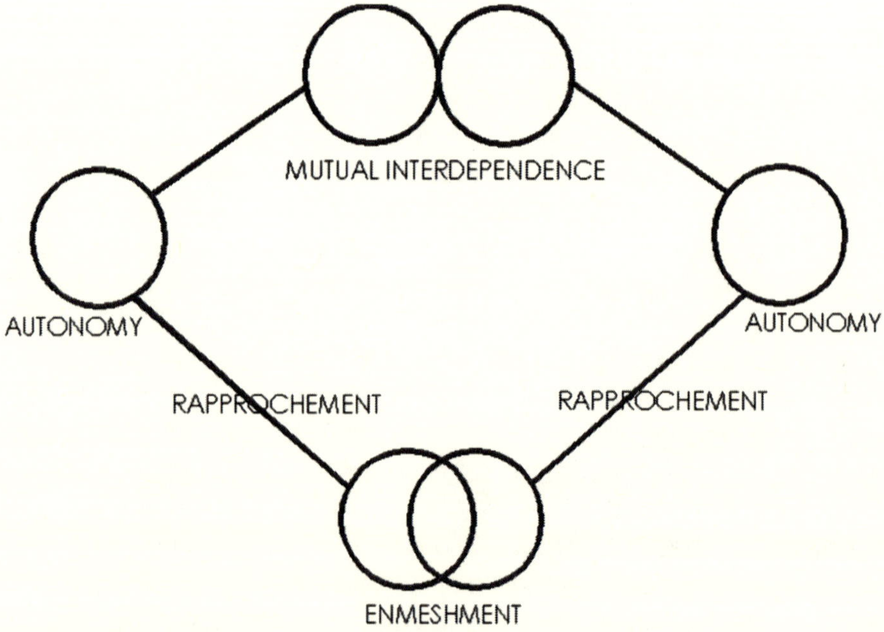

New relationships often begin in a state of enmeshment, that "falling in love" period when we want to spend every waking hour together. This can be a positive starting point that develops the container for the "energy body" of the couple. For some couples, this phase lasts a long time, and then the "honeymoon" is over.

When one person in the couple wants to move out and explore life on his or her own (take a class, spend time with friends), the other who is still in enmeshment may feel abandoned, rejected, and alone. He/she may create couple issues that will bring the attention of the other back into the couple arena. However, if the other person is supported to explore interests on his/her own, that person then enters rapprochement and continues to move toward autonomy. If both parties move toward autonomy, they can begin the journey to mutual interdependence, which is true intimacy. If, however, they are fearful of becoming enmeshed again, they may resist this movement.

It is important at all stages of the journey to support healthy development and to take risks to achieve each stage. Sometimes, when fear is present, one person moves in toward enmeshment and the other withdraws toward autonomy. It is important to understand that these movements are old strategies from early developmental separation anxiety. Bringing this into consciousness can help a couple move beyond fear into loving support.[1]

SEXUALITY AND THE SECOND CHAKRA

If the second chakra is the development of sensations, emotions, pleasure, and duality, then the expression of those qualities finds its home in the experience of our sexual or sensual energy. Sexuality combines movement, feeling, desire, and connection in a joyous experience of pleasure. As a force of energy, Eros moves through us, awakening our body, mind, and spirit to life and to love.

In western culture, sexuality is rarely talked about or studied in a conscious way. We are not raised to explore the sensations in our bodies joyously or to do so safely with others. We may do so by ourselves, but it is often seen as wrong or shameful.

With most traumatic experiences, we respond by shutting down sensation or dissociating from our bodies entirely. As adults, we look to intimacy to reclaim our right to feel, and once there, we often encounter blocks. Managing our sexual energy becomes a problem instead of a pleasure and an inspiration.

In many indigenous cultures, the art of sexuality is an essential teaching that usually happens at the onset of adolescence, in a rite-of-passage experience. Because sexuality is honored, a child's self-exploration of it is considered normal and the teachings about it are held sacred. This is one of the most common areas in need of healing. Because of our inability to embrace our sexuality as a culture, we often encounter its shadow in the form of rape, incest, impotence, infertility, unwanted pregnancy and abortion, and sexually transmitted disease. Some of these issues have reached epidemic proportions.

ARCHETYPAL ENERGIES OF THE SECOND CHAKRA

As we respond to the instinctual drive to manifest what we learn, we activate certain archetypal energies. These energies relate to our emotional and sexual development and our need to create. In the second chakra, we may find a variety of these energies at work. The Caregiver, whose main job is to love and nurture, may be active. The Lover, or any participant in a relationship (Student, Child, Spouse), finds its roots here as well. Certainly, the Creative One or the Artist finds support from the generative aspects of the second chakra.

It is primarily visualization and imaging that support the development of healthy archetypes and guides. These in turn form the symbolic counterpart to the physiological process of healing that merges body, emotions, and spirit. Because the second chakra works so much with our unconscious, it is most helpful to access the archetypal energies through nonverbal means, and we can do this with our imaginations. The qualities we have developed are supported by our symbolic life. We can call on our archetypal energies for support through the imaginal process for whatever aspects need attention.

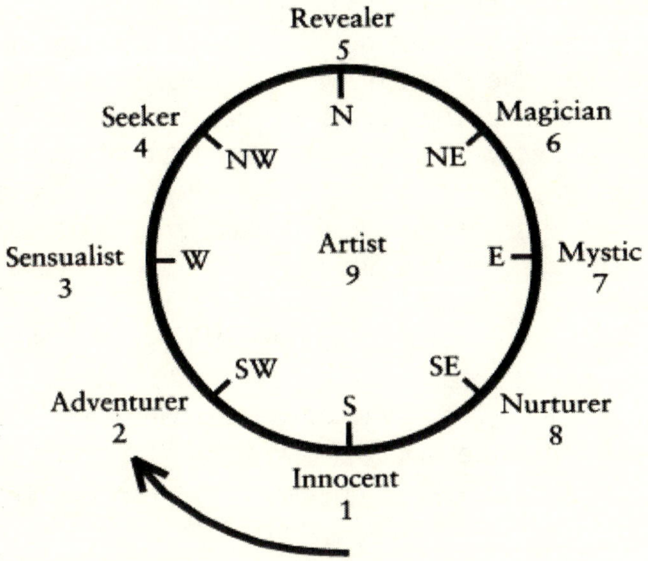

Wheel of Sexual Archetypes

© Mourier & Herriot 2003

A specific set of sexual archetypes and their relationship to each other is helpful in understanding some of these unconscious parts and our sexual nature. Using what sex therapist Oona Mourier calls the "Wheel of Sexual Archetypes,"[2] we can discover the available energies we utilize in the experience of our sexuality. This model, which uses the Native American Medicine Wheel as its structure, shows common archetypes and forms a developmental picture of how we move from the innocent (child) to the nurturer, or master of our sexual energies, in relationship.

Eight archetypal energies hold a place in the eight directions. At the center is the ninth, the Artist, who acts as the mover of energy and assists with the integration of all nine. Another way of saying this is that creativity is the generator of our sexual smorgasbord of experience.

The south, according to ancient traditional beliefs, holds the elements of water and emotion and the Innocent. Here, one is looking for information; one is exploring, curious. The Innocent in us is open with little judgment and is willing to try anything. There is no sense of containment or boundaries but fleeting energy. The Innocent is good at initiating but has no holding power or mature sexual energy. Above all, the Innocent wants safety and uses imagination and fantasy. The shadow aspect is the victim or wounded child. On the positive side, as we age, this archetype is about opening to new parts of ourselves. Often in relationships, we may find ourselves living in our Child archetype, which makes for unequal power. One strategy to change this is to find new archetypes in which both in the relationship are equal.

In the southwest lives the Adventurer. This is the adolescent part of ourselves that desires arousal and wants to try new things and break taboos. This is the age when we discover masturbation and sexual toys. There is often a lot of energy with no awareness of where it is going. The Adventurer has no mirroring, no set boundaries, and a lot of juice. There is no mastery here, just the willingness to try anything. The shadow side of the Adventurer is that this exploration is done without heart and the connections between partners do not run deep.

In the west, the realm of Earth and the body, lives the Sensualist. The Sensualist is comfortable in her body and enjoys the energy here. She is more mature than the Adventurer. She has solid boundaries, and she loves the sensations of physical pleasure and orgasm. She has the ability to let go and transcend into an experience where boundaries dissolve. On the down side, she is often caught up in her own experience and may trade safety for sensation.

In the northwest lives the Seeker. In this place of mystery and danger, there is a shift from the personal focus of the sensualist to a larger world. When we embody this archetype, we break away from tribal beliefs and enter a fantasy realm. We push edges and the dynamics of power and surrender. This is the realm of S&M rituals, where one holds the container for the other to journey into unknown parts of themselves. There is a conscious agreement here and a need to know oneself and one's boundaries. In this sexual exploration, we may journey into our wounding as well as our power.

In the north, the realm of air and mind, lives the Revealer. It is here that integration of the underworld experiences occurs along with the reorganization of the psyche. The Revealer is open to information from universal wisdom and learns the proper use of the mind. Our beliefs and thoughts affect our body image and contribute to the meaning we place on sex. This is where we make contracts or agreements about our sexuality. We ask "Who am I?" and "What do I want?" The shadow aspect is control and giving our mind more power than our emotions, spirit, or body.

In the northeast lives the Magician. This is where we design and choreograph our experience and where we give away our energy to someone else. Our wisdom and experience are used for the well-being of another. In this archetype, we share our mastery with others and act as healer for each other. Ceremony and ritual are often used for balance and empowerment. The shadow energy misuses this sacred trust and power for self.

In the east, the realm of Spirit and fire, lives the Mystic. Here, sexuality is about being one with the universe. Moving energy throughout the body is important, as are the teachings of Tantra and breath work that connect one with universal energy. One is comfortable being alone and experiencing fire, passion, and cosmic energy through the vehicle of sex, which catalyzes energy. The shadow aspect is being disconnected from the body, feeling ungrounded, and using the energy to transcend or escape the mundane world.

In the southeast lives the Nurturer. Here, we snuggle and rest in our intimate connections. This comfortable place is the foundation and container of long-term relationships. There is not a lot of sexual energy, but there is a lot of holding for other archetypes to explore. Because it is so easy to be here, some people get stuck here and feel no sexual juice.

In the center of the wheel lives the Artist. This is the archetype that is able to move from one direction to another and knows how to dance with the energy of each aspect of our sexual nature. The Artist spins the wheel and keeps us from becoming stuck in any single energy field. When we do feel stuck, creativity in any form will move us out and allow for new energies to emerge.

When looking at this Wheel, you can see how two people could find themselves in opposing archetypal energies and how, by moving to another direction, it is possible to break the cycle and renew sexual interest. It is helpful to identify which archetypes are already at play in you and which are below the surface or underdeveloped.

How we feel about our bodies plays a large part in how we explore our sexual nature. If we have had negative input about certain body parts, we can nurture the Revealer, Healer, and Nurturer inside ourselves to resolve it. If we are inhibited, the Adventurer, Seeker, or Innocent may support our desire to break out of old molds. If we tend to live in numbness, or have dissociated, and live outside our body, nurturing the Sensualist is helpful. And if we want an experience of interconnection with the cosmos, then branching into the practices of the Mystic is the next step. The guiding principle here is playfulness; make this a joyous experience.

CREATIVITY AND WORK

To expand our view of creativity—especially as it applies to life work or path—consider again the paths of Creation Spirituality: Via Positiva, Via Negativa, Via Transformativa, and Via Creativa. Chaos is an essential element of the creative process. Out of breakdown, shattering, falling apart, and confusion comes the inspiration to create a new form. The need to create is often born from a stuck place. We hit a boulder on the path or we find ourselves in an uncomfortable and scary part of the unknown, and we have only our senses to guide us. Our experiences are often painful. We feel the contractions of life. This is known as Via Negativa or the path of darkness and letting go.

In this part of the journey, we ask ourselves how suffering expresses itself specifically in our day-to-day experience. When we identify the origins of our pain, we can begin to identify the aspects of chaos present in our lives. It is not enough, however, to know what is wrong. To achieve expansiveness, we must also identify the wisdom and compassion (Via Transformativa) that we have gleaned from that suffering.

Sharing these with others allows us to come into communion—first about our suffering and then about our learned wisdom. When we share, we find that we are no longer separate or alone; others know our experiences. We remember we are all on a journey and there are steps to this journey that we all experience. This is "cosmogenesis," or the evolution or creation of wholeness.[3]

Let's look at an example. A child is born and becomes a part of a family. Her nuclear family is a part of a larger extended family; there is a new whole. That larger tribe is a diverse part of an even larger community, perhaps an ethnic or religious group. Each individual in the group is seen as a part of the whole, and that whole is now another complete entity—and part of a larger whole. This goes on and on until we reach cosmological proportions. Then the movement reverses so that within the immensity of our universe, we identify and act out our own unique articulation of life. Together with our ability to grow ourselves (autopoesis), we flow between the oneness and diversity in a dance of creation (Via Creativa). There is no value judgment, only movement, creativity, and an experience of oneness.

The conditions for creativity are usually disequilibrium, turbulence, and conflict. In order to enter that chaotic state, we must have a strong ego container with which we can experience a deep relationship with mystery. An inner sense of autonomy is essential so that we can let go to the creative process, allow for change (Via Creativa), and not be scared by it. Creative energy is the essential energy of the divine. In the Kabbalah, the Jewish mystical teachings, it is said that wisdom, understanding, loving kindness, and empathy are all creative energies of the divine.[4] When we enter the creative process, we are touching on the power of creator and must allow it to move through us. To that end, here are some suggestions for how to engage in creative process:

1. Trust that you are innately creative. The spark of divinity within you drives your creativity. Know your biorhythms; match your daily schedule with different kinds of creative endeavors. For example, if you are more active in the morning, do your creative work in the morning.
2. Experiment with different creative techniques. Honor your own creativity by setting aside time to create sacred space for it. Don't force creativity; eliminate blocks instead, like fear of failure or success and feelings of inadequacy. Relax into your creative self via a meditation practice as this cultivates relaxed alertness. Pray that your creative acts be gifts. Ask for inspiration, love, and compassion to accompany the process.

3. Invoke your muse. Ask yourself a question or give yourself an image, a movement, or a thought as a seed, and allow it to take you somewhere. Allow for incubation periods, relaxed times, dreaming. Ask yourself a question before sleep and notice how your dreams respond.
4. Leave the editing and changing until later to allow the free flow of creativity to emerge.[5]

RIGHT LIVELIHOOD

Just as we must expand our concept of creativity beyond the cultural definition of art making, we must look at work from a larger perspective to include every action that supports us. We still define work as survival, and we hold the tension of those survival issues in our second chakra. To transform work from actions of surviving to thriving, we must infuse it with our creativity and our spirit. All work is creative endeavor, and all actions of creativity can be work.

As we wake up to what truly sustains us, we begin to transform our sense of trust and guidance. With a strong sense of self and a solid connection to our creativity, we can risk trading old beliefs for new thoughts such as, "I can transform my work to suit my needs." Only by looking at our old beliefs from our tribe and culture can we begin the process of transforming such a powerful entity as work into right livelihood.

For most people, work is something we have to do to make money. Few people have work that is integrated into their life in a meaningful, fulfilling way. Doing work that has personal meaning for you, that serves you in some way, or which you love to do is the goal of right livelihood and the domain of the second chakra. Because we learn what is expected of us from our family of origin, we bring that information to bear when we choose work. If we were permitted to explore our creativity and passions, we tend to choose work that supports our growth. If we were taught we must work to survive, we will choose work that provides the basics without much thought for anything beyond it.

Thriving in work is an expression of thriving in life. As author Studs Terkel noted, to be authentically human, work must be "about a search for daily meaning as well as daily bread, for recognition as well as cash, for astonishment rather than torpor; in short, for a life rather than a Monday through Friday sort of dying."[6]

Doing what we love expresses who we are and provides a gift to others. Loving what we do brings us joy and energy. Doing what is expected or demanded of us without thought to what inspires or supports us can block energy. Blocked creative energy can lead to pain and illness in our second chakra. By reclaiming our right to feel not only our emotions but also a sense of truth or purpose in our work life, we naturally become healthier.

Theologian and scholar Matthew Fox has written that "we become real when our inner work becomes work in the world, when our creativity serves the cause of transformation, healing, and celebrating, when our work becomes compassion, expressed in creative ways that surprise and that effect change."[7]

The sacral chakra, then, is a multidimensional area that offers a wide variety of holistic understanding. From early development and relationships to sexuality and right livelihood, this area of the body-mind holds many experiences and opportunities for expansion and healing. It is truly the Fruitful Dark.

CREATIVE PROCESSES

I. ENTERING THE FRUITFUL DARK

Bringing your attention to the sacral or low belly area of the body can deepen your connection to what is hidden from conscious awareness. It is often sensed or felt emotionally but can remain mysterious. This is an opportunity to bring to conscious awareness through imagery that which is more underground.

MATERIALS

Meditative instrumental music
The Spiral of Healing CD
Art materials
Journal or other writing notebook and pen

MOVEMENT/VISUALIZATION

Begin by warming up the body. (See "Waking Up the Body," page 59.) Move in a flowing way to include all body parts. Focus on moving your hips and waist, your pelvic area and belly. When you have brought your awareness fully into your body, find a comfortable way to be and gently focus on your lower abdominal area.

Allow yourself to imagine a doorway into your second chakra area, either through the belly or lower back, whichever feels right to you . . . Step through the doorway, and notice that you are in a place where your ability to sense or feel leads all the other senses . . . It is very difficult to see or think like we normally do. It is dark and mysterious, like moving through the underworld . . . In this place, we generate ideas and life. It is the seat of creation within the body. It is also the place of elimination, of letting go physically . . . Emotionally, we are journeying to autonomy in our relationships, and we need to belong as we separate. Spiritually, this is the opportunity to receive, create, and let go. Here, we can connect with our passion and our energy to manifest . . .

Notice and sense qualities that exist here for you . . . Is there a heaviness, thickness, pressure? Does it feel light and airy? Is the energy moving quickly or slowly? Do you like focusing here? Sense the fruitful dark for a few more minutes, and when you are ready, come back through the doorway.

ART PROCESS: ENTERING THE FRUITFUL DARK

Image your experience using whatever materials call to you.

WRITING

Write about what you received in this process in your journal.

II. EMPATHETIC CLAY PROCESS

Here, you will have the opportunity to focus on one person who has a powerful presence in your life. The purpose of this exercise is to allow you to see your projections and understand more fully the family dynamic operating between the two of you. It is an opportunity to develop empathy and practice compassion.

MATERIALS

Two three-inch clay balls
Board
Masking tape
White unlined paper (12 x 18)
Art materials
The Spiral of Healing CD
Journal or other lined paper and pen

MOVEMENT/VISUALIZATION

Begin by warming up the body. (See "Waking Up the Body," page 59.) Move in a flowing way to include all body parts. Focus on moving your hips and waist, your pelvic area and belly. When you have brought your awareness fully into your body, find a comfortable way to be, and gently focus on your low abdominal area.

This process is best done sitting at a table. Begin by checking in with your body, and center yourself.

Write down any words and symbols that you have for divinity. Write down ten ways you define yourself—your roles and qualities. Read this list over, and notice the different facets of yourself that you have identified. In front of each word on the list, add the words "I AM."

Reread your list, and then repeat to yourself five times the words "I AM" with your eyes closed. Track the responses in your body. Open your eyes. If you are doing this process with others, make eye contact with someone as you continue to repeat the words you have listed preceded by "I AM," and track your responses. If you are alone, use a mirror and make contact with yourself as you do this.

ART PROCESS: EMPATHETIC CLAY PROCESS

Next, think of someone with whom you are in relationship who evokes a powerful response in you. You can choose whether this response is positive or negative. With the first clay ball, create a vessel for that person by imagining their interior life. Discern textures and forms that would manifest the interior life of this person as you imagine it to be. Include a symbol for the divine for this person. All of this goes on the inside of the vessel. On the outside of the vessel, image how that person presents him/herself to you and the outside world.

The second vessel is about you. On the inside of the vessel, add an image or images of how you feel in this person's presence. Include a symbol of divinity for yourself. On the outside of the vessel, portray how you present yourself back to this person.

As you make these vessels, notice any somatic (body) responses, and use the masking tape to mark your body where you feel it. This will help you see where and how your body is holding this relationship.

WRITING

Set the two completed vessels on a white sheet of paper in spatial relationship to each other. Let the pieces dialog with each other, and write it down.

Journal about the experience.

III. FEELING YOUR SENSUAL ENERGY

The following two movement exercises give you an opportunity to connect somatically with your own sensual energy and passion. Please take special care to create a safe environment when doing these.

MATERIALS

Meditative instrumental music (to be used during the process)
Art materials
The Spiral of Healing CD
Journal or other writing notebook and pen

MOVEMENT/VISUALIZATION I

Begin by calling in a witness, someone who loves you and will support your experience. Listen to "Waking Up the Body" or move in a flowing way to include all body parts . . . Focus on moving your hips and waist, your pelvic area and belly . . . When you have brought your awareness fully into your body, find a comfortable way to be and gently focus on your lower abdominal area. Scan each body part, and breathe into it, moving from your head down to your feet . . . Loosen your neck and jaw, and continue to move down, paying attention to sensations in each part, breathing, softening, releasing.

Lie on the floor with your knees bent and feet flat on the ground. Soften your body, and loosen your jaw by breathing slowly and sending warm energy from your head to your toes . . . Feel how relaxed you are.

Begin by slowly rocking your pelvis up and back, arching your back slightly, and curling upward . . . When your pelvis is up, your back is flat on the ground. When your pelvis is down, your lower back is raised a bit off the ground. These do not have to be large movements, just enough to get your attention.

Coordinate your breathing with the rocking . . . Relax your neck and jaw as you do this . . . Exhale as your pelvis comes up . . . inhale as you lower your pelvis down . . . Find the rhythm that works for you . . . As you breathe and do this gentle rocking, stay soft and loose.

Our center is located in the middle of our pelvic girdle. This is a great activation place, where a lot of energy passes through. If images or sensations come up, notice them, pay attention, be curious, and try to leave judgment out.

This is an opportunity to come into relationship with an aspect of yourself—your sexual body. It is like taking a walk with someone new, someone whom you want to get to know. This part of ourselves holds the key to our passion and our energy.

Stop the pelvic rock, and sense any feelings, thoughts, or images as you bring your awareness to your pelvic area . . . Be gentle with yourself and track your sensations.

ART PROCESS: FEELING YOUR SENSUAL ENERGY I

Image your experience using whatever materials that call to you. When you are finished, set the image aside, and return to the floor for the next part of the process.

MOVEMENT II

This movement uses what are called Kegel exercises—exercises that focus on the pelvic floor or perineal muscles. For women, this is the muscle between the anus and vagina. For men, this is the muscle between the anus and scrotum.

To begin, try to isolate these muscles from your anal muscles or sphincter muscles by consciously softening them . . . Next, tighten and release this muscle slowly . . . Be aware of any thoughts, feelings, sensations, or images that come in as you do these subtle contractions . . . Notice where your energy is blocked and where it is flowing . . . Continue to breathe gently and normally.

Take the opportunity to think of something you want in your life, something you are passionate about . . . It might be something you are studying or already doing. It might be a person or a connection to yourself. Whatever it is that excites you, turns you on, gets you going, call that in for yourself now . . . If you can't find anything, connect to the *notion* of passion . . . What would it feel like if you were so excited about something you could hardly sit still, if you woke every morning feeling alive because you got to be with this experience in whatever form it takes?

As you bring this in, do the Kegel exercises, and experience the sensation of what it feels to work your passion and your body at the same time . . . Tighten and relax those muscles, feeing the energy rising as you think about your passion . . . Breathe into your low belly and pelvic area . . . Let this experience move up your body, bringing compassion, curiosity, and attention to it as it moves . . . Let it travel through your second chakra . . . up into your solar plexus, the place of right action . . . up into your chest area, aligning your heart with your passion . . . up into your throat, to your expression, your truth . . . up into your eyes, to your place of visioning, thinking "I can do this" . . . and send it out the top of your head, giving it away to Spirit for guidance and help . . .

Repeat this, starting at your feet . . . moving the energy up through your whole body and finally releasing it out the top of your head . . . Then, from the top of your head, let guidance, wisdom, and anything that wants to come in about this passion inform you . . . Allow the sense of guidance to flow down, informing your sense of clarity (brow chakra) . . . your heartfelt nature (heart chakra) . . . your sense of self (solar plexus) . . . creativity (sacral chakra) . . . and manifestation (root chakra) . . . Feel your Kegel muscles again . . . Feel it coming into the Earth, into solidity.

Thank your witness who came to be with you . . . thank your body for speaking to you in its language . . . and thank yourself for your willingness to move into this arena.

ART PROCESS: FEELING YOUR SEXUAL ENERGY II

When you are ready, image any part of this experience that is meaningful for you using whatever calls to you. Let your body inform you.

WRITING

Journal about the experience.

IV. EXPLORING SEXUAL ARCHETYPES

MATERIALS

Meditative instrumental music
The Spiral of Healing CD
Art materials

MOVEMENT

Begin with "Waking Up the Body" (use prerecording, or see page 59).

Allow yourself to connect to one of the archetypes shown on the wheel (page 91) that is familiar to you in your sexual life . . . Recall a recent time when you enacted this role . . . Sense where in your body you feel this energy . . . How does your body hold this experience for you?

Look at the wheel again . . . What role did your partner play? Sense how that and any responses you may have had to your partner's role felt in your body.

ART PROCESS/WRITING: EXPLORING SEXUAL ARCHETYPES

Image these archetypes using whatever art materials call to you. Let them dialogue with each other. What relationship do you think they have?

You can draw or use clay to create the feeling of each one. Ask these archetypes in the dialog if they would like to do something else or be someone else. If your partner is willing, experiment with changing archetypes in your intimate life, and notice how you feel in your body. Sense any places of tension and relaxation as you explore new ways of being together.

V. ADDITIONAL EXERCISES FOR EXPANDING SEXUAL AWARENESS

1. Call in a quality that you need regarding your sexuality and breathe it into your feet and legs. Continue to breathe it into your low belly, solar plexus, heart area, throat, eyes, and head. Breathe another quality into each chakra. Again, notice your sensations, thoughts, feelings, and images as you do this. Track where your breath moves and where it stops. Image your experience using whatever materials call to you. Journal about your experience.
2. Draw an outline of your body on a large piece of paper. Go through your body, noticing the messages you have about each area. What is your body's response to these messages? What

would you have liked to have heard instead of the message you got. Change what you wrote to support and sustain your new and evolving relationship with your body. For example, if you heard "having a curvaceous body is bad," you might change that message to "my body is lovely just the way it is."

3. What aspect of you—physical, emotional, mental, or spiritual—most needs healing right now? Focus on breathing Earth energy into your body and surrounding what needs healing with Earth energy on the out breath. When you feel ready, image your experience using whatever materials call to you.

FURTHER EXERCISES AND QUESTIONS

1. Create and complete an "emotions chart" to fill out daily for one to two weeks. Chart daily all those emotions or sensations you experience, such as anger, contentment, depression, excitement, fear, joy, sadness, shame. Notice all the different ways you feel and how it manifests in your body. Look for any patterns as the days pass. This may help you to understand your feelings in a new way and expand your spectrum of emotions.
2. How connected are you to your creative energy? How do you define creativity for yourself? How do you manifest it in your daily life?
3. What survival issues do you have regarding work? What do you need to identify and transform so you can create work that nurtures and sustains you? What can you commit to working on immediately?
4. How does money have authority over you? Do you let your financial decisions compromise your inner self?
5. How does your work reflect the values of your tribe? How does your work express itself in creative ways that nourish you and that make a difference? What would you change about your work if you could? What practical steps can you take now toward that end?
6. How connected do you feel you are to your inner artist, lover, and caretaker? Image these archetypes, and dialog with them to

get more information on how to feel more connected to them. What would you change about these if you could?

7. Are you comfortable with your sexuality? If not, what would you like to change?
8. Choose a meaningful relationship, and chart where you and the other person are on the individuation diagram (see page 88). How do you feel about where you are?
9. Name a relationship in which you feel enmeshed. Name another relationship in which you feel autonomous. Name another where you have a sense of interdependence. How do you feel in each of these relationships? As you reflect on this, notice where you hold these feelings in your body. What would you like to change, if anything, about these relationships?
10. How comfortable are you in your sexual energy? Where in your body do you sense your sexuality?
11. Which of the sexual archetypes are you familiar with, and which are foreign to you? Which ones do you find yourself stuck in, and which do you avoid?
12. What would compassion look like in relation to your body?
13. Answer the following questions:
    My body is happier when . . .
    I feel better in my body when I . . .

14. Focus on what you feel grateful for about your body. Appreciate how far your body has taken you and what it has done for you. List three appreciations.

3.

TAKE ME TO MY LEADER

DISCOVERING IDENTITY AND PERSONAL POWER
Solar Plexus (Third) Chakra

Our deepest fear is not that we are inadequate.
Our deepest fear is that we are powerful beyond measure.
It is our light, not our darkness, that most frightens us.
We ask ourselves,
Who am I to be brilliant, gorgeous, talented, and fabulous?
Actually, who are you not to be?
You are a child of God.
Your playing small doesn't serve the world.
There is nothing enlightened about shrinking
so that other people won't feel insecure around you.
We were born to manifest the glory of God that is within us.
—Marianne Williamson

The energies of the third chakra, while connected to the tribal influences we find in first and second, begin the movement away from others and focus on the self. Located in the solar plexus region of the body, the third chakra develops the experiences of personal power, self-esteem, identity, intuition, will, and the archetypes of the adolescent, the seeker, and the warrior/leader.

Developmentally, we are moving into autonomy in the external world as we let go of dependency on tribal influences and begin the journey of discovering who and what we are, what is our purpose and path, and how we follow our own integrity. In this chakra, we reclaim the right to act and to bring forth right action into the world. It is the opportunity to honor ourselves as we begin to bridge the external worlds of the first three chakras with the internal worlds of the other four chakras.

When we are born into this life, it is said that we come from a place of oneness where we know we belong. We do not sense ourselves separately in the womb. We are then born and are completely separate; we are a little baby—unique and individual. We have to work with this dichotomy all our life: how do we find our uniqueness, and how do we belong? In the best of worlds, a young child gets an embodied experience of this by spending lots of time in nature and understanding and appreciating that he is a part of this beautiful creation. He is held in love and respect in his family, and he is allowed and encouraged to develop skills that tell him that he is a part of life and also unique. He knows that he has something to do here and is grateful for the gift of life and the need to give back.

SELF-ESTEEM

Some of us learn about love and respect while others get the experience that we are alone, isolated, and disconnected. Out of our childhood experiences, for better or for worse, grows the sense of self.

Before we can act with honor and clarity, we must feel a strong sense of self-esteem. This developmental task involves five aspects that cycle throughout our lives: a sense of safety internally and externally; a sense of belonging to something greater than ourselves; a sense of identity, both personal and global; a sense of competence in our actions; and a sense of purpose or path we are traveling.

Safety is the basis for a healthy self-esteem. Knowing we are safe allows us to take risks, to challenge ourselves, and to move through scary and painful experiences. Knowing we are connected to something greater than ourselves allows us to relax into our life experience. It helps us develop trust in our ability to make healthy choices. It also allows us to ask for help and come in communion with others in difficult times. If we do not feel safe, we will prioritize the need to find safety for the rest of our life.

Both safety and belonging promote a natural experience of identity. Within our boundaries, we can explore who and what we are, what we believe, and how we want to share ourselves with others. If we feel safe but do not feel we belong, we will spend most of our time trying to assimilate. We must feel accepted and acceptable in our tribe or we will feel like an outsider. If we are appreciated for our unique contribution to the family, we will relax and get on with the interesting tasks of growing. But if we do not feel appreciated, we will try to figure out how to get our needs met even if it means suppressing feelings or behaviors or speaking the truth. It is a more fundamental need to feel safe and belong than it is to claim our uniqueness.

When we feel safe and have a place in our world, we can concentrate on exploring who we are both personally and globally. We discover our relationship to our original family, community, and local area. At that point, we can recognize our connection to other life forms and to the planet herself.

We feel competent when we feel a sense of safety and belonging and know who we are. Feeling competent allows us to try new things, to risk making mistakes; we know we can learn from them. We can develop new skills, both internally and externally, and feel good about ourselves in the process. It's a positive cycle.

Finally, when we know why we are here or what we are here to learn and to offer to others, we claim a direction and a path to walk. To fuel our work in the world, we connect with our passion and our compassion. We come to terms with our universal connection and discover how guidance works in our lives.

While these tasks that contribute to our self-esteem are developmental (they occur over time), they can also be experienced cyclically. We can feel a strong sense of competence and purpose in some areas of our lives while in other areas we know relatively little about who we are. We are traveling the spiral path as we learn about self-esteem.

A good example of this is Simon who was in his thirties when he began the Spiral work. He grew up with an angry mother who needed him to serve her needs but could not reciprocate. She was unable to tolerate his unique creative self and squashed most of his attempts to be original and playful especially when he was messy. Early on, Simon got the message that his needs were wrong; and because upsetting his mother was terrifying, he stopped having any needs but served her instead. As he grew, Simon connected less and less to what gave him passion, and he had to hide whatever passion he did have from his mother. In adulthood, he struggled with fidelity as his need to be seen as lovable from many people ran his life. He struggled to manifest any of his creative endeavors even though he was a very talented man. Only when he began to connect with his body sensations and early traumas did Simon realize how this early parenting had affected his sense of self-esteem, and so he began to heal and change. He recovered his true connection to himself and others and entered into reciprocal relationships, both giving and receiving. He is working hard to manifest work that brings him joy.

IDENTITY

The experience of identity begins developmentally after rapprochement, when we come into our first experience of autonomy. We feel separate; we know we are something other than our mother. We may not know what that something is, but we begin to sense it.

For most of us, the real work of identity begins in adolescence as we reject the persona shaped by childhood and question what is true for us. We experience more of this when we leave home, join new communities, and/or go to college. In adolescence, we take on the energy of the seeker archetype and try on different identities and ways of being.

Once we feel connected to a strong self-esteem, we can undertake the tasks inherent in claiming our personal power. Having the ability to respond in situations is the true meaning of responsibility. Being a disciple unto oneself is at the core of discipline. These two skills are essential if we are to claim our power and feel autonomous.

Another important skill to develop is our intuition when we sense what Caroline Myss calls our "ability to use . . . the emotional, psychological, and spiritual components of a given situation to make decisions in the immediate moment."[1] We have a felt sense about something, and we listen to that sense. For the most part, we can identify the presence of intuitive information when we pay attention to our body sensations, when we feel uncomfortable, depressed, anxious, detached, or simply respond to a gut reaction. In dreams, we receive symbols of change that inform us. We follow our intuition when we shift, move, or take some action without our rational mind. Something deeper in us just knows what we must do, and we do it. Having a strong sense of self-esteem allows us to connect with our intuition and to trust it.

STAGES OF PERSONAL POWER

Creating an identity for ourselves in the third chakra is based upon self-discovery and not upon biological and cultural inheritance. To break away from family understandings and connect with our true selves requires that we move through four stages of personal power. These stages may happen in short cycles or be a matter of lifelong learning.[2]

The first stage is when we break away from what we have learned in our tribes and discover independent thinking. This usually begins in adolescence when we reject and separate from the thoughts of our parents and other authority figures. The act of finding our own voice can feel revolutionary and is spiritually significant. It expresses maturity and a courageous willingness to stand one's ground in support of a genuine inner belief. It is not rebellion for the sake of being different. It requires a willingness to let go of the known and venture into the mystery.

The second stage happens when we have pulled away from what we have relied upon and engage in discovery and learning. We go inward to gain information and strength. We assess the external world as it is and ask how it serves our needs. We ask self-reflective questions, and we gather thoughts of others and contemplate their truth for us. The first stage provided the space to do this. Now we begin the difficult task of discovering what we know and believe. With self-knowledge, we have the ability to choose well and to act.

Out of the introspection of the second stage comes a birthing of our self. This third stage reflects a healthy narcissism; we put ourselves first and create a new way of being in the world. This can include creating healthy boundaries, stopping old patterns of caretaking, and/or taking an unpopular stand. Narcissistic energy can give us the strength to recreate ourselves in the face of opposition. It looks at the world through *our* glasses, not any handed us by another. This is a very necessary step to autonomy. It is not uncommon in this stage to meet crises to test determination. Dynamics with others will also frequently challenge during this stage. Healthy narcissists will often be called selfish by those used to being put first by them. This stage therefore requires courage and strength to keep going and to balance the energies between self and others.

The fourth and final stage of reclaiming personal power is internal. It happens when we maintain our principles and faith without compromising our energy or losing our spirit. It is a completed evolutionary process. This is also the transformational stage when we have completed the task and begun the cycle anew. The butterfly has left the cocoon and has begun its life. In this stage, we no longer need to prove ourselves, act narcissistically, or be vocal. We simply live our experience, and we trust it is felt and respected by those around us.

ARCHETYPAL ENERGIES OF THE THIRD CHAKRA

We are living in our warrior/leader when we experience our personal power as a way of standing in the strength of knowing who we are. In our warrior/leader, we honor and respect ourselves and others. We align our words with actions, respect limits and boundaries, live responsibly and with self-discipline, demonstrate right use of power, and choose to show up and be present.[3]

Leadership is essential in manifesting the warrior/leader. The qualities of warrior/leader require that we be present, speak truthfully, be visible, know what we represent, and stand up for ourselves and others. To say what we mean and mean what we say promotes effective communication and the ability to be truthful.

Leadership skills always involve awareness. Identifying our pain and the pain in others leads to compassion. Asking what we can do to alleviate the suffering in the world and staying open to what is going on around us cultivate important awareness. It is equally essential to find a focus for transforming suffering and recognizing the light in all beings. Leadership skills allow the spirit to grow and to express itself in right action.

One aspect of the healthy warrior is what is known in spiritual literature as "the spiritual warrior." It is that aspect within that travails through life's challenges and stays connected to a greater awareness of life. As Matthew Fox describes it,

> "A warrior defends what is beautiful; a warrior defends Creation and its light; a warrior defends what the community cherishes; a warrior assists the community to survive. A warrior's heart must be strong but also creative; it must be connected to the whole; it must know quiet and solitude as well as busyness and engagement. It must be familiar with nothingness and it must have tasted joy. It must know service as well as sacrifice. In short, it must know spirit."[4]

Parents and educators are among the strongest examples of Fox's ideal spiritual warrior. They must be firm yet loving on a daily basis, often sacrificing personal needs for the safety and welfare of the children in their care.

> "A parent must do strong things at times, pay mindful attention, be alert, loving and defensive of one's children, protecting them from onslaughts from advertisers and media, communications that would distort a child's view of creation. Yet, a parent must also let her or his child go to experience life on their own. There is a special art to being a parent . . . an art that combines heart and head, love and intelligence, communication and silence . . . . An educator is a warrior, one hungry for truth, on the lookout for ideas that stimulate and excite, and put minds into motion. A true teacher finds rest in truth and joy and does not confuse learning with elitist education."[5]

A WARRIOR PRACTICE

> The warriors tame
> The beasts in their past
> So that the night's hoofs
> Can no longer break the jeweled vision
> In the heart.
>
> —*Hafiz*[6]

Finding the inner Warrior is synonymous with willingness to meet our inner demons and transform them. We do not have to fight them; we have to be strong in ourselves, have enough support, and have contact with our inner Warrior. Then, when we are confronted by old fears or traumatic response patterns, we can confront these and shift our relationship to them. If we are going to do battle with our inner demons, we must do so from a state of love.

There is no weapon stronger than love. We must be deeply connected to that which loves everything, which breathes life into everything, which generates the creative flow in us and in all life around us. Then we can meet any difficult energy and know how to work with it. This is the purpose of healing the old wounds of isolation and alienation.

This is our job: to get clear, to get present, and to get rid of what drains our power and energy so we are aware of our cocreative potential and ability. Then we are free to contribute to and create a world that works for all life.

One of the most effective tools for transforming old patterns is "The Autobiography in Five Short Chapters."[7] I call this a "warrior's practice" because it allows us to track our process from unconscious triggers to full awareness of our patterns. And it provides a step-by-step method for shifting old ways of operating.

AUTOBIOGRAPHY IN FIVE SHORT CHAPTERS

Chapter 1. I walk down the street. There's a deep hole in the sidewalk. I fall in. I am lost. I am helpless. It isn't my fault. It takes forever to find a way out.

Chapter 2. I walk down the same street. There is a deep hole in the sidewalk. I pretend I don't see it. I fall in again. I can't believe I'm in the same place, but it isn't my fault. It still takes a long time to get out.

Chapter 3. I walk down the same street. There is a deep hole in the sidewalk. I see it is there. I still fall in. It's a habit. My eyes are open. I know where I am. It is my fault. I get out immediately.

Chapter 4. I walk down the same street. There's a deep hole in the sidewalk. I walk around it.
Chapter 5. I walk down another street.

Remember the last time you fell into a hole? It happens a lot. The hole may be emotional, mental, physical, or spiritual. It can occur when something goes wrong with your body. There you are, minding your own business, and boom! You are suddenly in a dark hole. You don't know where you are. You don't know why you feel like you do. No one can tell you. You use all of your resources—draw on all the old strategies but nothing works to get you out. Even your sense of reasoning doesn't help. You feel overwhelmed. You feel helpless and lost. You may feel very young in this place. It seems to have hit you from out of left field. What is going on? You are re-experiencing early traumas or you are being triggered by old developmental blocks. Our nervous systems register this by immobilizing our responses. We freeze and have no idea what to do.

When you fall into this place, start by getting comfortable; you may be here awhile. First, look at the reason you fell into the hole. There is something you need to learn about the hole. Don't fight being here. Breathe into it, settle in. When you try to ignore it or pretend it is not there or that you do not feel this way, you only dig yourself deeper into the hole. Try a new way. Look around. Bring your creativity into play.

When you are in the underworld, as you are when you fall in that same hole, and you call in your creativity, you will discover the way out. Draw with pencils, colored pens, pastels. Sense your body; write in your journal. Help is available if we allow ourselves to sense those "dark feet and dark wings."[8] Using your senses, imagery, and your body and breath, you can learn to accept those uncomfortable and unrecognizable places. It is true that the only way out is through. By sitting with what is, instead of fighting what is, we can recognize what needs to change and learn how to do it.

Chapter 2 in the "autobiography" is about denial. This is not like the first time you fell in. That time, you did not see the hole. Now, you know the hole is there, but you pretend it is not. The first time, you were innocent. The second time, when you find yourself unable to avoid falling in, you feel trapped again, maybe even judgmental:

you should have known better! You minimize, rationalize, pretend this situation or person is not really triggering you, and that you do not really feel angry because anger is not an acceptable feeling.

You are a bit more awake, but you are still unable to handle or center yourself. So you do what is familiar. The old patterns and habits are stronger than your newly awakened consciousness about them. You see the hole, but you ignore it because you want what you want. Perhaps you still want that candy even though you know that every time you eat it, you will have a negative reaction. Or you notice you have chosen the same kind of person with whom you have unhealthy relationships, but you are starved for affection and attention, so you engage with them even though you know they are not good for you.

In Chapter 2 we have an inkling of what we want, but we do not trust our intuition yet, so we go for what is familiar. We are caught in a pattern, an addiction. Because of this, we still need to be in the hole so we can learn more about the habit in which we are caught. To get out, we need to be more creative, more open to understanding our part in the drama.

In Chapter 3, you begin to take responsibility for the habit. You have all the information you need. Let's say you keep falling in love with the same kind of person. They look good on the outside, but the moment you get comfortable, they get scared, or they overwhelm you, or you do not feel heard. In Chapters 1 and 2, you put the issue onto the relationship. In Chapter Three, you own it. You realize you are doing it again. You recognize this is your issue and you need to do something about it right away. You'll take action. Maybe you will leave the relationship. Maybe you will get support or speak your truth.

This is a great place to be on the warrior's path. You are in touch with who you are, and you can feel your core, your power. You can still get triggered; that is an experience of being human. You are allowed to miss things and make mistakes. But you are not allowed to stay there and grovel in it, to let it beat you up because now you know better. You know this is not about anyone else, it is about you. You get help, come back to yourself, and bring yourself back into integrity. You do whatever you need to do, and you get out of the hole.

Chapter 4 is the beginning of a new way inside of a familiar context. We ask ourselves why we cannot speak our truth, and we reclaim our abilities. We honor the old and claim our feelings about it. We pull back the projections we've put onto others, and we own our process as part of the journey to wholeness. We learn to sit with ourselves in the emptiness and ask for help. When we work with an issue, like not being heard in a relationship, we name it. We have compassion for ourselves and appreciation for all the players for what they are teaching us. When you meet someone you are attracted to, you may make a choice not to pursue your attraction because you see your pattern and you know it is dangerous. Or maybe you decide it's time to soften your stance when you talk with your daughter or son. Whatever it is, when you notice the potential for a trigger, you consciously choose to do something else.

In Chapter 1, you have figured out why you needed to be in the hole, and you don't fall in the hole again. You choose a new street. Here, you stay clear of old reactive patterns and recognize when you feel something in the present moment that is not actually happening. You understand why you have chosen relationships that do not nurture you. You see the payoffs and how they supported your old strategies to feel safe or to belong. You can move on and walk down a different street.

SHADOW ASPECTS OF A WARRIOR/LEADER

When we encounter the shadow archetype of the Warrior, we come face to face with the obstacles to our innate capacity to empower ourselves and others. Often, these take the form of fear of misusing power, lack of self-esteem to claim our gifts and talents, and the inability to find our autonomous adult energy, which can carry the responsibilities of the Warrior.

There are several key aspects of the shadow Warrior/Leader to acknowledge and transform.[9] The first is the Rebel who breaks away from the norm but does so without honor or respect. The Rebel needs space and fears restriction or limitation, often acting for personal gain. While some Rebel energy is important, it needs to be balanced with effective leadership skills that empower and honor others.

A second roadblock to healthy personal power is giving away our energy to others, projecting our authority onto someone instead of claiming it for ourselves. If something goes wrong, we can blame it on someone else. This unwillingness to claim personal responsibility for our lives can lead to victim mentality. When we own our personal power, we are no longer a victim and can engage with others who demonstrate effective leadership skills.

The third shadow Warrior (living with unclaimed personal power) hides or holds back, engaging in patterns of invisibility. When we do this, we cannot see ourselves as we truly are and cannot accept our power and gifts of creative expression. These shadow Warriors are afraid of exposure and accountability and hide behind other powerful people while believing they are in their own power. Their fear keeps them small when their souls are crying out to be of service.

A true Warrior embraces all aspects of the journey and summons the courage to move through these obstacles. The Warrior also recognizes a fourth shadow aspect—the abuse of power or misdirected love energy of the third chakra.[10] This is often seen in negative behavior among adolescents, who are just beginning to feel their power in the world. When we support teens to come into their power through healthy and observable rites of passage, to own his or her strength and purpose, the teen will grow and thrive. The community must support the process, or power can and will be taken through any means necessary.

In this stage of development, we must become who we are, and anger is often the first way to experience our power. Transformation of that anger into right action is the challenge and the prayer. Again, this is part of the warrior's work—to uncover our true identity. As Matthew Fox describes it, to do this Warrior's work is:

> "to be strong in who we are, who we are becoming, what we stand for, and the values that call us forward into new places and new roles. In short, to find our true center."[11]

In South Africa, there are people who work with the shadow Warrior in a unique way. When a person of the Babemba tribe acts irresponsibly or unjustly, all work ceases, and every man, woman, and child in the village gathers in a large circle around the accused individual at a location in the center of the village. One by one, each person in the tribe speaks about the good the person in the center of the circle has done in his lifetime. Every incident, every experience that can be recalled with any detail and accuracy, is recounted. All of his positive attributes, good deeds, strengths, and kindnesses are recited at length. The ceremony often lasts several days. At the end, the tribal circle is broken, a joyous celebration takes place, and the person is symbolically and literally welcomed back into the tribe. The value of this practice is to help the person see beyond his mistakes. The tribe reminds him that he is more than his shadow.

SELF-WORTH AND SELF-CRITIC

There are times when we feel good about ourselves, when we know our value and our importance in the world. Then we run into another part of ourselves, the part that many have identified as the internal critic, which knocks us off our center with judgmental thoughts. That critical voice becomes a part of our internal cast of characters.

Try asking yourself if "the good, true, and beautiful within you is as strong as the whispers of diminishment."[12] In other words, is your self-loving nature as obvious and strong as the self-judgment? Are the two in balance? If you could invite these two to come together, to interact, how would they behave? Would one take up all the room? Who leads, and who follows? What is the power dynamic between these two? Who do you pay more attention to?

The calm, centered, quiet power in our third chakra, the home of our self-worth, supports the Warrior/Leader. There, we know about the important relationship with the critic. We know we need the skills of discernment and focused attention that come with critical thinking. We need the power that comes with the critic; when it shows up, we jump to attention. Self-worth is not an oppositional force to the critic; we need them both. But we must live with a proper balance between them.

Finding healthy ways to promote self-esteem and personal power in ourselves and in our communities is essential to transforming injustice and oppression. The right use of power supports human development and diversity.

CREATIVE PROCESSES

I. FIVE ASPECTS OF SELF-ESTEEM

In this process, you are invited to sense and image your relationship to safety, belonging, identity, competency, and purpose as you live now and in relationship to work, play and interactions with others.

MATERIALS

Meditative instrumental music
The Spiral of Healing CD
Art materials
Journal or other writing notebook and pen

MOVEMENT

Start with "Waking Up the Body" (use CD, or see page 59). Turn on the music, and begin by moving your body to its rhythms. Feel your energy move as you sway and gently begin to move your body. Take your time, and allow your awareness to stay with your breath as you move through your body.

GUIDED VISUALIZATION

Find a comfortable position, and allow yourself to begin to sense safety in your body . . . You might find yourself in your safe place image or in another location that you know as safe, or you may simply notice what sensations move through you as you visualize yourself free from harm . . . Allow others into your safety realm . . . Allow any images, colors, or textures that invoke the feeling of safety for you to emerge.

Notice how your body responds to the experience of belonging . . . Recall in what situations you feel connected with others and feel this bonding in your body . . . Allow any images to emerge that support this feeling of belonging . . .

We'll now work with your sense of self. How do you identify who you are? Let yourself create a picture of your sense of identity as it is today, and allow that picture to drop into your body . . . Where does it land? How does it feel to know who you are and what you are about? Sense any feelings, thoughts, and images that support your present identity . . .

Where in your life do you feel competent? What talents and skills that enhance your feeling of competence do you have or are you developing and learning? Locate this sense in your body and allow any image to emerge . . .

Finally, sense in yourself the reason you are here . . . What is your purpose in this life, and what steps are you taking to achieve this? Sense this in your body, to the best of your ability . . . How is your purpose being shown to you in thoughts, feelings, sensations, activities, images?

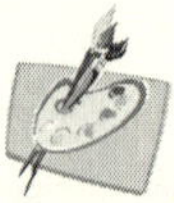

ART PROCESS: FIVE ASPECTS OF SELF-ESTEEM

When you are ready, create five separate images, each one representing one of the five aspects of self-esteem: safety, belonging, identity, competency, and purpose. These can be a symbol or a complete drawing.

WRITING

Work with each image separately, dialoguing with it and noticing how you feel when you look at the image.

When you have completed this first writing, link the images together in some way so that they make one image that represents a totality of your sense of self-esteem. Again, sense the totality in your body. Respond to the image either by writing, dialoguing with the image verbally or by doing a movement that allows you to feel each aspect of your self-esteem. Feel the connections among the five aspects as they now have created an entirely new entity. Appreciate your wholeness.

II. EXPLORING PERSONAL POWER

This movement and art process invites you to feel yourself in different situations where you experience several aspects of power: under, over, and empowered. It is an opportunity to sense how you move through space and time and image your personal connection to power.

MATERIALS

Meditative instrumental music
The Spiral of Healing CD
Art materials
Journal or other writing notebook and pen

MOVEMENT

Begin by walking around the room at a normal pace. Notice your breath, the position of your head, and how your feet move on the floor. As we change qualities of movement, remain conscious of what happens to your body and your breathing.

Walk as if you have no time and too much to do . . . You are harried and overextended . . . Notice what changes—like speed, breath, what's constricted, the position of your head, and especially your thoughts and feelings about being so harried and busy . . . After a minute, shake that off and resume normal walking . . .

Next, walk as if you are aimless, drifting along, with no purpose or destination . . . Again, notice the speed at which you move and how your breath and body respond to this quality, the position of your head and your thoughts and feelings . . . Is this comfortable and familiar, or do you have judgments about it? Is it "lazy" or not permitted? After a minute of this, shake it off and resume normal walking.

Walk as if you are purposeful but relaxed, having a destination but comfortable with your gait and timing . . . Notice whether you feel light or heavy, where your head is now, how it feels to move in the space . . . If this is not familiar movement, track the sensations in your body's response . . . Resume normal walking.

Walk as though you are feeling overpowered, out of control, and at the effect of someone or something else . . . Notice your movement, whether it is free or stifled . . . What is the position of your head? How is your breathing? Where do you feel constricted or relaxed in your body? Shake that off.

Now walk as though you have total power over others and you are overpowering to others . . . Imagine someone in front of you whom you can overpower, and allow yourself to feel this sense in your body . . . This may be difficult, but allow yourself a moment to fully sense this quality. How does your body respond? How is your breathing, your posture when you are overpowering others? Shake that off.

Finally, allow yourself to sense that you are in charge of yourself and comfortable standing in who you are . . . You feel empowered . . . Walk with that knowledge and experience . . . How does this feel in your body, and how is it different from feeling overpowered or when you overpower others? Spend a moment in this quality and then come into stillness, noticing how your body is speaking to you.

ART PROCESS: EXPLORING PERSONAL POWER

Image your personal power with whatever art materials call to you.

WRITING

Dialogue with the image. Write your experience of these exercises in your journal.

III. SELF-WORTH AND SELF-CRITIC

This process is an opportunity to experience the connection between two parts of yourself: the part that judges and the part that unconditionally accepts and supports you. These two parts are in relationship in almost every aspect of life, and it is important to sense how they interact. By bringing awareness of this, you will be more at choice around, listening to the inner critical voice.

MATERIALS

Meditative instrumental music
The Spiral of Healing CD
Art materials
Journal or other writing notebook and pen

MOVEMENT

Start with "Waking Up the Body" (use CD or see page 59). Turn on the music, and begin by moving your body to its rhythms. Feel your energy move as you sway and gently begin to move your body. Take your time, and allow your awareness to stay with your breath as you move through your body.

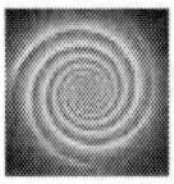

GUIDED VISUALIZATION

Pay attention to your breath . . . As you breathe in, notice where your breath moves in your body . . . Get comfortable, and breathe out anything you don't need for the moment. Let go of extraneous thought . . . Breathe in softness . . . openness . . . breathe out what is in the way of feeling open.

Bring your attention to your solar plexus with your hand or awareness . . . Focus on your intuition and the knowingness that comes from this part of you . . . With your soft attention on your third chakra, imagine a portal or doorway . . . When you are ready, step through this entryway until you find yourself in a realm, on a path, and notice what is around you . . . Notice colors, textures, temperature, sound, whatever is there . . . Be aware of all the life moving around you.

As you meander on this path, become aware of that companion who sometimes travels with you, the one with focus and clarity and judgments, the one who is quick to tell you what is wrong . . . It is referred to as the critic, the judge, even the predator. Be aware of the presence of this energy, walking not too close but not too far away, in constant focus and movement . . . The critic is always working. Notice in yourself when you become aware of your critic's existence. Perhaps you turn to the right or left or hear a sound or word, and notice what happens in your body . . . What is your response when you are with the critic? (Take plenty of time to sense this.)

On the other part of the path, the other side, away from the critic, is another energy that is beginning to take shape or form or texture or color. This energy is the energy of solidity, of knowingness, of contentment, of calm and quiet, of compassion and love and great clarity . . . When you turn your attention toward this energy, new feeling begins to emerge within you . . . What do you sense in your body when you are near the energy of acceptance and balance . . . of expansiveness . . . openness . . . And there may be other qualities that come with this energy. What are they? Invite this energy to walk with you on the path, play with it, and notice what happens to you . . . Give yourself plenty of time to drink in this being. If it has a form, notice what form it takes or what colors surround it, and begin to engage in a conversation with this part of yourself . . . What does it want to be called? Ask it whatever you want to know . . .

Now call in the critic to join the two of you . . . Notice the three of you together . . . Notice how your energy flows into the critic and how it flows into your self-worth or the one that is connected to the source of your power . . . Allow the three of you to engage in some form of communication . . . Perhaps there is a way you dance together or talk together . . . Use our imagination, and find the thread that ties you all together . . . Discover the purpose these energies have for you . . . There is no right way to do this; whatever happens is perfect in this moment . . . When you have gained some sense of the energies and their relationship with each other, walk back through the doorway and gently move your body.

ART PROCESS: SELF-WORTH AND SELF-CRITIC

Create two images, one for your self-worth and one for your critic. Allow yourself to personify these energies so you can enter into a conscious relationship with each of them. Then bring the two images together in some way to show their relationship to each other. If you are using three-dimensional materials, like clay, find a common environment to put them in together and align them in such a way that you can sense their relationship within yourself. If you are drawing, cut them out and put both on a third piece of paper and draw their relationship.

WRITING

Let the images dialogue with each other about an issue that is pressing for you, and write that down. Journal about your experience.

ADDITIONAL EXERCISES AND QUESTIONS

1. Of the five aspects of self-esteem—safety, belonging, identity, competence, purpose—which is the most challenging for you right now? What wisdom have you gained from reflecting on these aspects in your life?
2. Where in your life do you stand up for yourself? In what circumstances and with whom do you lose a sense of personal power?
3. Looking at the four stages of personal power, describe where in your life you experience revolution? Involution? Healthy narcissism? Evolution? How do you feel about these stages? Is one more comfortable than another?

4. Of the qualities of the warrior/leader, which are you strongest in and which are challenging to you?
5. Of the shadow aspects of the leader, where in your life do you stay invisible? Where do you rebel? With whom do you have authority issues?
6. How do you support yourself to be responsible, respectful, honorable, and disciplined? How do you respect the boundaries of others as well as yourself?
7. What are your associations with power? Make a list of words you associate with power. Notice which are positive and which are negative.
8. What is the relationship between your sense of self-worth and your self-critic? Which is stronger? How do you respond to your critic? How do you sense each in your body?
9. Imagine a situation where your inner authenticity does not match your outer communication. Redo this so they are congruent. What qualities do you need for there to be this congruency?

4.

HOME IS WHERE THE HEART IS

LOVING AND NURTURING SELF
Heart (Fourth) Chakra

To study our own hearts is to rediscover longing.
Longing brings up fervor, an intense desire
to be with the object of our longing.
To reject longing . . . is a way without creativity,
a way without passion.
—Matthew Fox

As we move away from group dynamics, we begin to explore our individual experience. Here, we come to the heart of the matter, our core. The fourth chakra lies in the center of the chakra system, with three chakras below and three above.

In our exploration of the first three chakras, we paid attention to group energy, to one-on-one relationships, and to ourselves as we move in the external world. We focused on our past, our mysterious creativity, and our exploration of authenticity. We explored the right to have, to feel, and to act. We moved through childhood and the archetypes of the Child, Lover, and Warrior. We worked with the senses of safety, belonging, and identity.

Now we turn our attention from the external reality to the inner journey. The fourth chakra is the balancing and connecting point between the lower chakras and those of the neck and head. Just as the keystone holds two sides of an archway together, the heart is the link between the lower and upper chakras.

Developmentally, in the fourth chakra, we are separating from the external impact of our early life as we face our inner motivations and inner wounding. The fourth chakra is the arena for the Healer archetype, for love, self-acceptance, and compassion. Here, we look at the relationship between self-loathing and self-loving, between caring for others and self-care. Physically, this is the area of the chest and upper back, with the breasts, lungs, and heart as the focus.

The fourth chakra invites us to pay attention to what has heart and meaning. It is a passion center. When we allow ourselves to be guided by our heart, we come into ourselves in a new way. We reclaim the right to love.

LOVE AND FORGIVENESS

As we begin to live from the fourth chakra, we realize we carry unique emotional perceptions and challenges. Our thoughts, ideas, attitudes, and inspirations move us in new and exciting ways. The challenge in the fourth chakra is to love ourselves, to have the courage to experience compassion and self-acceptance as part of the journey toward wholeness and spirit. What we encounter are the obstacles to that: past experiences of betrayal, grief, negative self-image, abandonment, and abuse that convince us we are unlovable and unable to create the life we want. We drop into our wounding and identify only with what is wrong with us. As we judge ourselves, we judge others and we remain separate and alone. Projection becomes the only reality, and we get lost in our own expectations.

Love is a form of divine power, which we learn about in early childhood through loyalty and support, and as we grow, through friendship and partnership. As adults, we pour our love into people and things, like our family, home, work, and activities. When we turn inward, we are challenged to embrace love of self, of all that we are, and especially of our spiritual journey. We ask the questions "Who and what do I love?" and we work with the issues of reclaiming the right to fully embrace our ability to love. This requires a great deal of self-forgiveness for all the ways we have not met our own expectations.

Matthew Fox writes that "our whole perception of reality changes when our heart changes. For this to happen, we must forgive; we must let go of remorse."[1] It also means we release ourselves from past traumas, no matter how difficult. We must see that the choices we made in childhood were creative solutions to abnormal and difficult situations, and we need to let go of the guilt or shame over having made those choices.

Some coping strategies that resulted from those early decisions directly affect our ability to love and care for ourselves. For many of us, if we could not get our needs met as children, we learned how to care for others and suppress our own needs. We become enablers, codependents, and unhealthy caregivers. We are seen but only in this regard and not for all that we are. We care for others at the expense of our own needs and accept ourselves only in that capacity. When we try to put ourselves first, we are engulfed in a sea of guilt and are challenged by our own grief for not being seen. We must learn to forgive ourselves and begin the uncomfortable process of focusing on our needs. Only when we forgive ourselves can we begin to let go of our anger and grief toward those who were unable to give us what we needed.

When we begin this journey, we usually bump headlong into our wounded self. We have to feel our grief from betrayal, abandonment, and other traumatic experiences and come to terms with the core beliefs we hold because of those events. These may include beliefs such as "I am not good enough," "life is hard," "I can't get what I need," "I don't deserve to feel good," "something is wrong with me," "I'm bad."

When we travel through the underworld of our pain, it is important that we hold onto practices that balance us. Resources such as art-making, singing, movement, and meditation practices, which encourage silence, can support our difficult journeys. Acknowledging the whole truth about ourselves, not just the old core beliefs, and speaking gratitude for all we have helps us maintain our focus; opening to the energies living in our heart helps us acknowledge, accept and give gratitude for the experiences that have made us who we are today. When we feel the guidance of our inner Healer, we begin to pay attention to our passion as well as to our pain and to work toward transforming old patterns into new actions. Only by learning to love ourselves with acceptance, patience, and compassion can we begin to give and receive love.

THE REALM OF THE HEART

The heart is like a garden. So much is growing there—beauty and nurturance, weeds that do not belong, and old growth that was planted ages ago. It is our greatest gift to know this garden and to be able to care for it appropriately. It is especially important to know when to pull the weeds and old plantings that are no longer needed to protect or cultivate the rest of the garden.

In the natural world, in the soil are the nutrients, the underground, moist, dark, mushy ingredients that feed the blossoming of the flowers. The flowers that grow in this garden trust that they will receive all that they need in order to flourish. They are in harmony with the thoughts of the garden; they resonate with the energy of life around them. In spring, they have to struggle to push through the hard ground after a long winter of incubation. With passion and persistence, they break through with small shoots of new growth. This is not an easy experience but one that is deeply embedded in their cells. It is the autopoetic way: they become all they are.

So too our heart must open, trust, and accept what life gives us. In the best of all possible worlds, that garden is rich with love and attention, appreciation of the uniqueness of each blossom, and a commitment to nurturing continual growth. When we do not get that, thorns grow, weeds take over, and through our determination to survive, we put in plants that seem able to help protect us and keep us safe. These plants grow tall and gangly, sometimes barring the sunlight from reaching the sweet little blossoms that are trying so desperately to grow in such difficult conditions. The passion so deeply a part of each plant is stinted or covered over by hardier plants that can grow in any environment. No one comes to move the soil, to clear away the harshness from harming the delicate blooms, to water and love the potential so lovingly held within each flower.

This is often the condition of our hearts when we begin to wake up and realize that we need help, that we are unhappy, that we cannot love ourselves or anyone else, or that we have no access to our feelings at all. The heart is meant to live in harmony with our head and our body. The heart is the part of our physicality that works tirelessly, pumping blood and nutrients to the rest of our body. It has a built-in mechanism to rest and replenish itself. It is the center of our being, our physical body, and our emotional and spiritual life.

Our language reflects this with such phrases as "knowing something by heart," "having a heartfelt response," "having the heart of a lion." These statements refer to qualities we value—embodied intelligence, compassion, and courage. They speak to our relationship with some energy that connects us with the rest of life.

The energies that are alive in the Heart chakra—which physically includes the breasts, lungs, heart, thymus gland, and upper back—are love, openness, acceptance, trust, harmony, passion, and compassion. The focus is the healing of old hurts and traumas and the movement from self-loathing to self-loving. When we are disconnected from ourselves, we cannot appreciate or accept our struggles and triumphs. Life is hard, rigid, negative, and dry. Not much can grow in these conditions. We must do something to change our situation.

Our birth experience leaves us with a dilemma. We must figure out how to hold the tension between our state of separate uniqueness and our longing for oneness. We do this when we experience love and creativity. When we know love, we are immediately connected, united in an atmosphere that is at once safe and pleasing, energizing and calming, comforting and enlivening. This is a spiritual or mystical experience, which most of us first taste in relationship with another person.[2]

For several months, I worked on an art piece for the purpose of healing an old wound and restoring the energies of the third and fourth chakra to their healthier state. The following poem speaks about my journey of recovering a truly precious part of myself—my heart.

I Am The Garden I Seek

I walk, sometimes I crawl, through shrubbery and thorns
To the center of my garden.
Here I notice the smells and rustling wind, the weeds and dry places.

I look for new growth and composting mulch,
the thirsty places and the quiet.
Being here requires getting down and dirty,
moving soil, pulling weeds.
When I've been away,
I see that it grows and changes whether I'm here or not.
But how much more beautiful and majestic when I linger.

How long has it been
since I've wandered through this luscious growth,
a day, an hour, six weeks?
No matter . . . I am here now,
sitting in the center of the garden I seek.
Amazed at the many rounds and cycles,
at the hard work I do when I'm here
pulling weeds, watering dry spots,
composting old growth
to protect and replenish what is just beginning.

I look over and see the old root I recently pulled.
It has taken a lot of time and effort
to move it out of the center of the garden.
It was so entrenched, so familiar
and it had so many other plants growing out of it.
Now it joins the rest of the compost
to be recycled as food.
Reminding me of what no longer needs to grow here.
I am handling the old root,
putting it where it can do the most good.
I am sitting in the center of my garden,
planting and cultivating
right where I am.
This is my garden.
Actually,
I am the garden I seek.

—Meagan Pugh

THE HEALER ARCHETYPE

Healing is a lifelong journey toward wholeness. It is the ability to change wounding into gifts, pain into knowledge, blocks into breakthroughs. It requires we accept that in all transformational processes, we must go into the darkness, that we must enter the fearful places we do not know about in order to reclaim lost parts of ourselves buried there. We must learn to be present with ourselves no matter what we feel and to let those difficult feelings guide us into creativity and transformation. As Fox says, "Creativity requires the darkness as well as the light, suffering as well as joy."[3] The same is true for healing.

If we can approach our healing with gratitude and connection to love, we will travel where we need to and come out the other end. We have access to the upper-world of spirit to guide our way, the underworld of mystery to wake us, and the middle-world of resources to support our journey.

To engage in the healing process is to love ourselves. It is to acknowledge that something is wrong, that we need help, and that we have the courage to face the truth in our lives and embrace our paths.

In any stage of our healing journey, it is essential that we accept ourselves. It can be hard to be in the process, to not already have arrived where we want to be. But the fantasies of an outcome rarely even begin to approach the wondrous reality of the experience we can receive when we relax into the process. The gift of healing is in the experience: at the center of the wounding is the healing; buried under the pain are the jewels.

Sometimes, we forget to look inside ourselves for the answers we need in our healing. We spend time instead looking to others to "make us" feel better. Feeling better is something no one can do for us. It's up to us to ask for healing, up to us to be open to receiving it in whatever form it will come. When we let go of the script for how it "should" be, let go of expectations, we become present to the gifting here for us all. We can trust what is given. There are blessings along the way. The journey is as valuable as the destination.

THE SHADOW ASPECTS OF THE FOURTH CHAKRA

What obstructs our ability to accept and love ourselves is, in part, the way we stay addicted to our history by continuing old behaviors that once served us. While there are many forms to these behaviors, I want to touch on four addictive strategies that inhibit healing.[4]

The first is the addiction to intensity. People with this addiction have a low tolerance for boredom. They need extremes to feel alive. They are typically unable to live and love in the mundane world. These are the people often called the drama queens and drama kings, those who require chaos or pain to sense themselves. Drugs, alcohol, and sex are frequently used to increase the sense of intensity, but the intensity is an illusion. The addiction to intensity usually reflects early developmental trauma, especially the lack of healthy boundaries and the freedom to explore safely within those boundaries. What is waiting to be reclaimed is the conscious expression of love and passion that channels potential energy into healthy creative ventures. As Fox points out, "Addictions come from our surrendering our own real powers of creativity . . . . Creativity takes courage and trust to explore one's deepest self, to go beyond what is known into the mystery."[5]

The need for perfection is the second common addiction that prohibits healing. It does not tolerate mistakes; it does not allow for learning curves. Vulnerability is seen as a weakness, and self-judgment runs high. With perfection our goal, our basic humanness is denied and our ability to learn from our mistakes is thwarted. We lose touch with the child in us who is vulnerable to awe and wonder, who makes messes, who has what Buddhist's call beginner's mind.

Perfection is the shadow side of excellence and right use of power. When we gain the leadership skills of listening and are open to outcome, we can soften this response to life and open the channels to healing. Another way to counter this rigid addiction is to change our beliefs about vulnerability and openness by examining our cultural myth about rugged individualism and embrace our mistakes as stepping stones to excellence.

> We begin life gentle and yielding.
> At death we are rigid, inflexible.
> The grasses that grow are green and supple.
> In death they are withered and sere.
> Therefore, the rigid and inflexible belong to death.
> The gentle and yielding are filled with life.
>
> —*Tao* [6]

The third addiction is the need to know. While it is important to be informed and aware, it is the addictive quality of this knowing that is stifling. The compulsive need for understanding can mask issues of control and lack of trust. If everything needs to be controlled, strategized, and compartmentalized, we can become dogmatic, righteous, critical, arrogant, controlling. To ease this addiction, we can allow ourselves to find comfort in the mystery. When we relax into *not* knowing and even feel good about it, we can be more objective, have greater clarity, and be more discerning. We can begin to develop a new sense of the world. In this process, we reclaim wisdom and gain tools for transformation.

Choreographer, writer, and cultural whirlwind Agnes de Mille writes that "living is a form of not being sure, not knowing what's next or how. The moment you know how, you begin to die a little. The artist never entirely knows. We guess. We may be wrong, but we take leap after leap in the dark."[7]

The fourth behavioral addiction that can stand in the way of healing is being fixated on what is not working. Seeing the glass half-empty leaves no room for gratitude. When we magnify negative experiences, blow them out of proportion, and view life from a fixed perspective, we are unable to trust our intuition or recognize our blind spots.

Life is a gift. There are lessons in all of our experiences, and it's important to recognize those lessons. Gratitude comes from our awareness and receptivity to the blessings that surround us. When we see the glass half-full, we begin to recognize just how much our lives *do* work. This allows us to reclaim our perceptions, insights, and visions for the greater good. It is a much sweeter way to live life.

The heart is the center and the core of who we truly are. It connects us to all of creation. The healing journey of the heart can bring us to a state of wholeness within ourselves. The fourth chakra energy embraces both the external and internal pathways and allows for the unification of the whole being.

As we deepen our healing journey, we come to rely on the information we gather from the heart and trust its message. By opening up to love, we open to ourselves and to all of life. With courage, we can heal. With love, we can overcome any obstacle.

Hold on to what is good
Even if it is a handful of earth.
Hold on to what you believe
Even if it is a tree that stands by itself.
Hold onto what you must do
Even if it is a long way from here.
Hold on to life
Even if it is easier to let go.
Hold on to my hand
Even if I have gone away from you.

—Pueblo Blessing[8]

CREATIVE PROCESSES

I. ENTERING THE REALM OF THE HEART

Like in other chakras, this process takes you deep inside your own heart energy to discover what is there. Again, there are no right or wrong experiences to have; it is more important to be open to receiving the gifts from your heart.

MATERIALS

Meditative instrumental music
The Spiral of Healing CD
Art materials
Journal or other writing notebook and pen

MOVEMENT

Begin with "Waking Up the Body" (use CD, or see page 59). Take enough time to bring your attention to each part of your body, connecting and awakening.

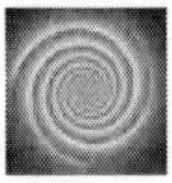

GUIDED VISUALIZATION

When you are finished moving through your entire body, bring your attention to your heart area . . . Become aware of any sensations in your upper chest, upper back, heart, lungs, and breasts . . . Pay curious and nonjudgmental attention to these sensations . . . Notice any imagery or color as you feel your body.

Allow yourself to connect with any anger, grief, fear, sadness, betrayal, or hurt that may be moving through you now or is unresolved from the past . . . Perhaps these feelings correspond to particular sensations . . . Notice the connection you make between these strong emotions and your body.

Continue to pay attention to your fourth chakra, this time noticing any thoughts that may be connected to particular sensations or feelings . . . Do you have any "shoulds" about yourself? Notice any self-loathing thoughts or statements that come as a result of focusing here.

As you concentrate on this area, what do you notice about your ability to stay connected to heart energy, to love? Are you compassionate, self-accepting, and able to forgive yourself?

ART PROCESS: ENTERING THE REALM OF THE HEART

When you have completed the visualization, choose an art medium that calls to you and image the condition of your heart in any or all of the above areas.

WRITING

Journal about your experience.

II. SELF-FORGIVENESS

The opportunity in this process is to become aware of some thought, deed, action, feeling, or attitude that makes you feel guilt or shame when you remember it. Sensing it in your body and then imaging the steps you would need to do in order to accept and forgive yourself is both healing and necessary. Pay particular attention to the critical voices inside that want to punish yourself for whatever it is you are working with. You may have to dialogue with them to find a solution that works for everyone within you.

MATERIALS

Meditative instrumental music

The Spiral of Healing CD

Art materials

Journal or other writing notebook and pen

MOVEMENT

Begin by turning on the music with "Waking Up the Body" (use CD, or see page 59).

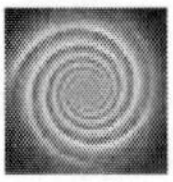

GUIDED VISUALIZATION

What would you forgive about yourself if you could? What do you feel you cannot forgive yourself for? Consider for a moment how you carry these beliefs in your daily actions as well as in your body posture and coping strategies.

You made some of your decisions when you were very young, when you had little information and may even have been in danger. Imagine yourself being young and making a choice that in reality you had no other choice to make . . . See yourself now as an adult holding and soothing your young self who had to make this choice that has affected you to this day . . . Together, agree to release any anger, shame, and self-recrimination for the decision you made.

ART PROCESS: SELF-FORGIVENESS

Using whatever materials call to you, create an image of your self-forgiveness.

WRITING

Allow the image to speak to you. Dialogue with the image. Journal your experiences. Allow your little one to speak as well, giving him or her plenty of room to write about the climate in which the original decision was made. What would self-forgiveness feel like if you could give this gift to yourself? Let the image help you sense it in your body.

III. ADDICTIONS

This process brings you into the awareness of four addictions: intensity, perfection, the need to know, and to what is not working.

MATERIALS

Meditative instrumental music
The Spiral of Healing CD
Art materials
Journal or other writing notebook and pen

MOVEMENT

Begin by turning on the music and listening to "Waking Up the Body" (use CD or see page 59). Try Gabrielle Roth's *Endless Wave* (see Audio Resources). "Body Parts" guides you through your entire body.

GUIDED VISUALIZATION

Take a few moments to center yourself after you have moved all of your body parts . . . Allow your attention to drift in your body as you think of your connection to the addiction to intensity . . . Where in your life do you strive for the edges, for the highest or lowest experience because it makes you feel alive? Think of a time when you felt bored . . . and remember what action you may have taken . . . As you feel the boredom moving through you, where is it most difficult for you to stay in contact with your breath or body? How long can you stay connected to that sensation before you want to move or think a new thought? Sense how your body contracts around the notion of feeling deadened.

Allow yourself to focus on your connection to perfection . . . Think of something recently that you wanted to complete—a project, a communication, anything that demanded a lot of your energy . . . Notice your responses to possibly not getting it perfectly right or what you may have had to do to make it perfect . . . In relation to your work, your healing journey, your connections to others, can you be messy, feel human, make mistakes? Or do you feel pressure to do it exactly right, whatever that means to you? What are your expectations of yourself? How do you feel about the last art process you did? Notice your breath and the parts of your body that tighten and constrict when you think about trying to accomplish something . . . What is your comfort level with not knowing? Think about something you want to learn, and sense in yourself how you feel about the unknown. What happens in your body as you focus on trusting without knowing?

Allow yourself now to sense the mystery of life and how much you do not know . . . Because the nature of reality is that we cannot control it. Sense that loss of control in your body . . . Where and how do you respond in your body when you realize that you are at the effect of so much around you? Sense the parts of you that "need to know" and cannot . . . How do you feel about the mystery or void?

Next, consider what you feel is "wrong" with your life . . . Think of a few specific situations and people who are not giving you what you need . . . Notice how your body responds when you think of this, when you feel the glass half-empty . . . While focusing on what is not working, begin to walk around the room . . . What do you notice about your energy, your posture, and your overall feeling? Still walking, remember one situation or person you are grateful for, and notice what changes in your body . . . Appreciate yourself for one action you have taken recently that has supported your journey . . . Again, notice what you feel as you walk around the room and how you feel in your body . . . What is different?

ART PROCESS: ADDICTIONS

Create an image for each of the addictions you considered in your visualization using whatever art materials call to you. You may want to ask each image what it might need in order to soften and image those responses. Sometimes, putting the softening agent around the original image can change the sensation in your body.

WRITING

Dialogue with the images, asking what each needs in order to change. Journal about your experience.

ADDITIONAL EXERCISES AND QUESTIONS

1. Spend five minutes each day doing cradling work. Place your right hand over your heart and your left hand over your right hand. Then either acknowledge your strengths and talents, acknowledge what qualities of character you like about yourself, acknowledge the contributions you have made and are making, and/or acknowledge the love given and the love received. Do this while looking at yourself in a mirror or with someone else.
2. Give one appreciation to someone you care about every day. If it is someone you live with (partner, child, parent, friend), do it at bedtime. This will ensure a deep and contented sleep.
3. In order to survive, what parts of yourself have you had to reject? What aspects are you working on to reclaim and reintegrate into your life?
4. Of the four addictions, which is most developed in you and where do you have the most experience?
5. What do you need to forgive about yourself? What do you need to forgive in others? How are these connected?
6. Where in your life are you compassionate and with whom? What aspects of your life do you judge or not accept?
7. Who and what do you love?
8. How do you experience divine love?

5.

SPEAK NOW OR FOREVER HOLD YOUR PEACE

RECLAIMING YOUR AUTHENTIC VOICE
Throat (Fifth) Chakra

What we speak
Becomes the house we live in.
Who will want to sleep in your bed
If the roof leaks right above it?
Look what happens when the tongue
Cannot say to kindness, "I will be your slave,"
The moon covers her face with both hands
And can't bear to look.
—Hafiz [1]

As a child living through a high degree of trauma, I learned to live by the adage "Don't see, don't feel, don't say." This translated into coping strategies that kept me alive but disconnected from myself and the world around me. I learned not to see what was before me and to discount what my gut and intuition registered. I closed my heart and numbed my body so I could get through each day without dissolving. And I learned very effectively to say only what others wanted to hear and to stuff the unpleasant but truthful words.

What we speak becomes the house we live in, and what I heard spoken around me created a house that was dark and full of demons. It has only been through the spiral journey of healing that I have reclaimed myself and the ability to see, feel, and speak.

LOOKING BACK ON THE JOURNEY

As we continue to explore ourselves on *The Spiral of Healing*, it is important to review the journey thus far. In the first few chapters, we identified archetypal energies, developmental challenges, and psycho-spiritual issues associated with the first four chakras of our body. We identified imaginal processes to explore our early experiences and our creative potential.

In the sections "Setting the Stage" and "Help Is On the Way," we reviewed the spiritual, psychological, and creative foundations of the spiral journey. Fundamentally, we began the process of creating a new relationship with our bodies, minds, emotions, and spirit. By engaging the body directly, we discovered and created resourceful relationships with ourselves through imaginal processes like the self-portrait, the safe place, the shield for boundaries and protection, and the Inner Healer Guide.

In Chapter One ("Laying the Foundation"), we explored the first chakra, the base of the spine down to our feet, as we looked at aspects of the Child archetype, including the Innocent, the Orphan, the Saboteur, and the Prostitute. We identified some of the ways we cope behaviorally with early stresses. We saw how primary family, community, and early experiences impacted our growth in terms of human needs like survival, belonging, and security. Those needs supersede individuality at this developmental stage and help us to receive, both negatively and positively, the tribal ethics of loyalty, honor, trust, justice, tolerance, and sexuality. It was those early core experiences that developed the beliefs and self-concepts that last into adulthood. In reviewing these early experiences, we have the opportunity to reclaim our right to have, to know what we want, and to retrieve and celebrate the spiritual truth that "all is one." Most importantly, we learned that getting creative and making messes grows a healthy child, and learning to develop self-awareness and competency heals early wounds.

In Chapter Two ("Entering the Fruitful Dark"), we explored the energies of duality, emotions, creativity, work, and sexuality that are living in our abdomen and lower back. This is a multilayered area full of subconscious or somatic activity where intellect is subordinate to sensation and feeling. Here, we take what we learned from our community experience and apply it to our individual relationships. Developmentally, we begin the journey of individuation and experience the rapprochement stage of practicing our autonomy while being witnessed and held in our attempts. We meet many challenges in claiming our life force energy, our sexuality, and our right livelihood.

Through creative processes, we encountered sexual archetypes and the Artist and the Caregiver archetypes. The challenge of the second chakra is to learn how to separate while keeping connected in our relationships and to develop a full palate of emotional experience. By focusing on our emotional capacities and our relationships, we learned to further the journey to autonomy and mutual interdependence. Here, we have the opportunity to reclaim the right to feel.

In Chapter Three ("Take Me to My Leader"), we accessed the energies of identity and personal power in the third chakra, or solar plexus area, of our body. We learned that the qualities of self-esteem—safety, belonging, identity, competency, and purpose—are lifelong experiences. We learned to honor ourselves and to recover the right to act in authenticity. We explored the archetypes of the Adolescent and the Warrior as we tried on different identities and practiced standing in our own truth. The challenges of the third chakra include accepting our power and learning to use it wisely. We distinguished the Critic and saw it apart from our self-worth, and we creatively learned how to identify triggers and avoid repeating old patterns.

In Chapter Four ("Home Is Where the Heart Is"), we explored the right to love and nurture ourselves. Here, in the heart chakra, we have the opportunity to heal old wounds and to forgive our early survival choices which no longer serve us. Through imaginal processes, we learned to appreciate our gifts and talents, to forgive our human limitations, and to develop compassion for ourselves and others. We learned about the heart as a garden, requiring tending and nurturing to thrive. We reclaimed the right to love and to recognize that love is a divine gift, which further connects us to our creative flow. As the center of our being, the heart acts as the conduit between the lower and upper chakras and houses the archetype of the Healer. We are invited to embrace our passions and turn our self-loathing into self-loving.

Figure 6—CHAKRA RELATIONSHIPS

1st and 5th	Early self-concepts and survival with self-expression
1st and 6th	Early experiences and core beliefs, rigid thought
2nd and 3rd	Willingness to choose and taking right action
2nd and 5th	Control issues in relationships and development of will; early traumas and inability to speak
3rd and 7th	Autonomy and sovereignty, right use of power
4th, 5th and 6th	Aligning what has heart and meaning with will development, expression and visioning

RELATIONSHIPS AMONG THE CHAKRAS

As we travel next into the upper three chakras, it is important to see connections between each one and where we have been previously (see chart below). I alluded to a connection between heart, throat, and mind (chakras 4, 5, and 6) when I wrote about feeling, speaking, and seeing. As we venture into the fifth chakra, it will become obvious how self-expression connects to survival and early self-concepts (chakra 1), how development of will begins with control issues in relationships (chakra 2), and how the willingness to choose relates to right action (chakra 3). Each chakra acts as a foundation for the next, forming the interrelatedness that is the coming together of mind, body, and spirit. The journey is full of gifts we discover we always had.

When we embody our experience and release the demons of our past, we sense the true nature of life, which is love. As we travel into the upper chakras and encounter the powers of speech, sight, and wisdom, let us remember the foundational experiences of community, relationship, and autonomy and witness for ourselves how the spirit dances us in new ways.

RECLAIMING OUR VOICE

Learning to reclaim our voice is a wondrous process of self-discovery. To do this, we have to first understand what has been lost and why. We live in a culture that discourages speaking up and reminds us of the consequences when we do. We are ostracized from communities when we point out injustice or offer a differing opinion from the majority. We are taught that "children should be seen and not heard." Even at weddings, we are asked to "speak now or *forever* hold our piece." Women are silenced more severely than men, but in general, we all are discouraged from protesting or pointing out problems within the status quo. It is no wonder the thought of speaking our truth is met with trepidation.

Our ability to speak is the domain of the fifth chakra, which is located in the throat, neck, mouth, esophagus, and parathyroid glands. This area has a unique relationship with our second chakra, both physically and energetically. Birthing women in indigenous cultures, for example, are encouraged to make sounds because an open throat helps the cervix open so the baby can pass through. During an intimate encounter, the kiss begins the neurochemical reactions that produce pleasure and orgasm.

The fifth chakra is where we take in nourishment. We chew, swallow, and begin the digestive process that moves nutrients throughout the body. We cannot separate body from emotions or parts of our bodies from each other. We are a single living organism, fully connected and interactive. It is our awareness that has been disconnected, not our bodies. That awareness can make all the difference between feeling open and being able to speak up or feeling constipated and unable to digest. When small children eat something toxic to their system, their peristaltic action reverses, and they immediately vomit; they have not yet learned to live with toxicity as adults have.

In this phase in *The Spiral of Healing,* we look at the information, emotions, and responses we have historically had to swallow and consider how we can identify and respond to such toxic energy now. In the fifth chakra, we communicate through sound and speech, learning to balance self-expression with listening. In this way, we keep the fifth chakra open and flowing.

Singing and chanting are used in many cultures around the world for health and wellness. Most spiritual practices include singing and praying aloud. Our first communications as children are the singing and humming of mothers to infants or the soft music of lullabies in the background while we sleep. We are an oral people, and we are created to communicate verbally.

With early trauma, speech patterns are often arrested. Young children who are abused, overpowered by narcissistic parents, neglected, or abandoned can suppress their language skills and, in some cases, become mute. The trauma is experienced as so overwhelming it cannot be communicated without a sense of disintegration, and so we stop trying to communicate. Children and adults need safe situations where they can begin to reclaim their voices, connect feelings with words, and learn to articulate experience.

COMMUNICATION AND SELF-EXPRESSION

Through verbal and nonverbal cues, we learn to express ourselves in the world. Children learn to speak by listening and looking. They watch their parents' body language and facial expressions, listen to their tone of voice, and connect these with the spoken words. If they are in alignment, the child can register meaning clearly and, after a time, can repeat back words, tone, and expressions that convey emotional learning. If we are fortunate enough to grow up in a family that encourages the exploration of language and feelings, we become comfortable in this arena. We practice conversation as we grow, and through trial and error, we become skilled communicators. We know that mistakes are how we deepen skills and expand vocabulary.

If we were taught as children that some forms of speech are off-limits, if our natural exuberance is unacceptable, or if we are shamed and ridiculed when we make a mistake, we learn early that self-expression is dangerous. Through body language, words, and tone of voice, we pick up what is acceptable to say and, by association, to feel. Our early self-concepts are formed around these experiences. It is not uncommon to feel inadequate or discounted or that no one wants to hear or see us.

Because of this early shaming, we can feel unacceptable as adults and project those feelings on others by using words that divide, judge, and disempower. We can do this in our workplace, with our children, and in our social circles. We take it out on other species and the Earth. If we have had to chew, swallow, and digest toxicity from a family or society that breeds distrust or if we have had personal traumatic experiences, we may be impacted in our ability to respond appropriately to difficult situations. Self-expression is as important as food, clothing, and shelter if we want to be productive in our lives and in the world. Our ability to communicate our innermost truths and feelings is as essential as being able to repeat back learned knowledge. It is part of our growing competency as adults to speak our truth in all situations. We need to learn how to speak up for ourselves, express a full range of feelings, and speak out against injustice. To do this, we need safe ways to explore and retrieve the gift of communication. In doing so, we heal.

Communication is an art form that requires practicing at two levels. The first level involves the intention to speak, to get out what wants to be said. It is often accompanied by a release of blocked emotion that is held in the body. Whether it is a withheld feeling, like anger or deep love, or an expression of pain or sadness, the risk to speak up is the possibility of misunderstanding or even rejection. While it may not be said perfectly or cleanly communicated, at least it is out. Repressing thoughts and feelings clogs the energy flow of the throat area and can lead to disorders and illness. At the very least, it will feel like hiding, which reinforces disconnection. To release tension and let the fifth chakra open, try allowing yourself to release loud sounds from deep within the body in a safe context. Some of the creative processes in this chapter can help with this.

The second level is learning to express your thoughts so that others can hear what you are saying without feeling defensive. One can feel relief and joy from speaking up, and the key is finding the words, tone of voice, and body language that will be well-received. Skill develops as we practice speaking our truth and learn to say what needs to be said without blaming or judging others.

Our original desire to speak up evolves into the desire to be heard. We begin to consider elements of right timing, content, and context. It is important that the person we want to speak with is ready to hear us. Finding a good time for both people is important to promote a relaxed environment. Getting clear on what you want to say and connecting your thoughts to an important theme (like harmony and cooperation rather than revenge or punishment) will also help the other person receive the information. We also begin to practice owning our feelings and thoughts and not projecting them onto others. Useful here is using "I" statements instead of "you" statements. With "I" statements (not "you made me feel" but "I feel") we take responsibility for our thoughts and feelings, and we are heard more easily. "I" statements provide room for another to receive content without feeling blamed or attacked.

Effective communication also requires developed listening skills. We have to listen to what others are really saying or are trying to say and not project our own beliefs about what they mean. The easiest way to do this is through a practice called "interviewing," or "active listening." In this way, you clarify what you are hearing, you develop your ability to listen, and you strengthen your ability to respond.

The next time you are in an important conversation with someone, particularly if there are emotions that could obscure clear communication, try this technique. First, ask for details about the statement they have made. For example, if someone says, "I hate it when you shout at me," ask them to describe how your shouting at them makes them feel. This lets the other person know you are really hearing them and are interested in what they are saying. Ask what they noticed about your body language when you shouted. This will help them identify triggers for themselves and help you become more aware of your delivery. Listen to what they say, and see if you can begin to empathize with them. Be curious about what is being said. See if you can imagine the issue located across the room from you and then look at it together. This can help you feel connected with the other person and allow you to approach it as a team instead of as adversaries.

Next, repeat back what you have heard each time something is said. If you need to, ask the person to slow down so you can hear everything said. Let them know they are heard, even if you do not agree with what they say. You might say, "I heard you say I scare you when I raise my voice. Is that right?" Allow them to qualify what they mean or tell you what you heard is correct. Letting them know they are being heard and validating their experience in this way always softens the dialogue and enhances communication.

Communication is a two-way experience. After one of you has inquired and the other responded, trade positions. Let the one who spoke first become curious and repeat what he or she has heard the other say. This trading-off slows down reaction time and directs the intention of the conversation to solving the issue at hand.

THE DEVELOPMENT OF WILL AND THE POWER OF CHOICE

The throat chakra is positioned between the heart and mind and through speech acts as the main focus for spoken communication and the development of will. A harmonious balance between heart (passion) and mind (thought) affects the expression of our will. When we lack heart energy, we approach whatever we are doing without a strong commitment. If our hearts are not aligned with our thoughts, we let "shoulds" control our passions and repress our feelings. If our emotions dominate our thoughts, we can lack the clarity to manifest what we want. In order to manifest our will, we need true balance between heart and mind.

As children we develop will by making choices. We first experience will coming from the authority of our parents, who provide limits, which gives us some sense of safety. Our young needs are best served when parents take charge and protect us from harm. With limited choices given us, we learn the consequences of our actions in safe ways. For example, when we have to choose between two toys or two sweaters, we learn about focus, priority, and letting go; when we choose one, we lose the other.

As we mature, we develop a sense of self that is separate from our parents. We come to understand that the authority is within us and, with wisdom, we choose for ourselves and experience the results of our choices. We begin to recognize how our will affects others and understand that we must honor and respect the burden placed upon us as we gain command of our will. When will is motivated by fear and control and not by a sense of internal security, we can lapse into behavior that is harmful.

Eventually, we may begin to be able to surrender our personal will to a sense of divine will. True authority comes with knowing that we are part of a greater whole. We can make choices that reflect that understanding as we learn to follow our intuition and guidance and trade personal agendas for the greater good. Given the opportunity to open the gates to our self-imposed prisons, we can recognize that will is one of the gifts of a flourishing fifth chakra.

PROJECTION AND ITS PITFALLS

One of the most significant misuses of will is a psychological concept called "projection." Projection happens when people fail to see another person as they truly are because their need for this person to be different or act differently than they are is so strong. Projection like this usually occurs because of early unmet needs. Back then, we had to push away parts of ourselves and our needs that were unacceptable at the time. In order to see these disowned parts or characteristics now, we project them onto someone else. As a result, we miss seeing the person as he or she truly is and we do not honestly engage with them. Instead, we connect with the projection we have placed on them. We do not get to our truth within the relationship because we are not having a relationship with the person in front of us. When we are aware that we are projecting, we can reclaim the projections for ourselves. The following is an example a couple who experienced this scenario in their family.

> Ruth complained that Ted did not honor all the work she did with their three children and their home, as well as her part-time job. He was raised traditionally and expected Ruth to do all the housework and child-rearing and not complain about it. Having a part-time job was for her and not for him or the family as it took her away from attending at home. He worked hard every day and didn't expect to be honored for that. But he also felt he didn't need to help with the house or kids either. From his perspective, that is just how you lived. Ruth and Ted were unhappy, not getting what they wanted out of their marriage, and so were unwilling to appreciate each other's contribution to the family.
>
> Both were operating out of unmet early childhood needs. They were raised in traditional households with large families, absentee fathers, and overwhelmed mothers who didn't

work outside the home. As children, their personal needs were discouraged in order to keep peace with everyone. As adults, both saw the other as the one who would finally attend to their needs, but neither had the awareness or skill to step outside of their projections and appreciate how hard each worked. They had projected their resentment of their parents onto each other and at the same time projected the good parent as well. So they were doubly disappointed when either person could not fill the "shoes" of the projections.

When they were able to see how they were missing each other by viewing the projection, they began the process of healing their own childhood needs and learned how to support each other to do so. This provided a healthy spaciousness between them that allowed them to be more present and to appreciate each other.

The best synthesis of taking back projections and reclaiming personal will I know was presented by poet Robert Bly. The Five Stages of Projection[2] that he outlined are below.

Stage One. This stage begins with looking around to find the perfect person to hold our projection. In this stage, we never see people for who they are; we see only what we want them to be for us. We may, for example, idealize someone who is powerful if we have not owned our power. If we have trouble expressing anger, we may notice and feel uncomfortable with those who can.

Stage Two. The projection begins to slip. We begin to see that the individual may be something other than what we have projected; however, we rationalize and excuse the behavior because we do not want to believe the projection isn't true. Taking someone off the hook for having a bad day, for example, allows the projection that has begun to slip to be put quickly back into place. You may think someone is wonderful and nurturing and loves you no matter what, and when they lose their temper, you minimize their emotion by justifying it. You may say they are tired and not thinking rationally when, in fact, you may have done something to stir their anger. You justify it in this way because you cannot accept anger from a person you think is always above that.

Stage Three. The projection falls off entirely. No rationalizations can be made. We are forced to see the person beyond what we projected. In this stage, we become disappointed, angry, blaming, and judgmental. We either move to Stage Four or find someone else to carry the projection and begin again at Stage One.

State Four. We recognize we held a projection and that it was our own material. This is a stage of grief. Here, we grieve the lost part of ourselves that has been away. We grieve that we did not see the other person for who he or she was. We see the unintentional harm we may have caused in Stage Three.

Stage Five. We feel compassion for ourselves and others with similar issues as we integrate the projection. We model the quality we once projected and carry no charge for what we once projected.

Reclaiming will through this powerful process is both healthy and important for the continuation of the relationship. Once we can identify our own needs for projection, we will more easily find the unmet need under it and take responsibility for meeting it ourselves. This releases the other person to be human. Then we can get to know who the person really is and have a genuine relationship with someone.

CREATIVE PROCESSES

I. EXPLORING YOUR THROAT CHAKRA

This process provides an opportunity for you to bring your awareness directly to the throat area and sense what is there. Imaging what you experience deepens your connection to the sensations.

MATERIALS
Meditative instrumental music
The Spiral of Healing CD
Art materials
Journal or other writing notebook and pen

MOVEMENT

Begin with "Waking Up the Body" (use CD or see page 59) . . . As before, gently move, breathing and focusing momentarily on each part as you travel up your body to the top of your head . . . Return to the throat area, focusing on the area from your ears to the top of your shoulders . . . Notice any sensations, emotions, or thoughts as you pay attention to this area . . . Relax your jaw and neck . . . Get comfortable sitting, reclining, or standing.

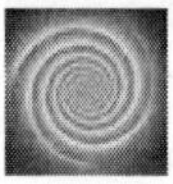

GUIDED VISUALIZATION

Allow yourself to imagine that in this area of your body, there is a doorway or entry point . . . Notice what the doorway is made of and how you pass through it . . . In your imagination, let yourself move through this doorway . . . As you move through it, you will find yourself inside a space that surrounds you completely . . . It is as if you have shrunk to a tiny size and are deep inside your throat, mouth, or neck area . . .

Sense this area now from the inside . . . Notice any color or texture . . . Allow your imagination to give you any image . . . How do you feel being inside your fifth chakra? Is it open? Loose? Closed? Is it tight or thick? Heavy or light? Get curious about the space you are in, and notice any thoughts or feelings about your fifth chakra . . .

Think about a situation where you need or want to speak out, to speak up and tell your truth to someone. See yourself in front of that person and about to speak. Take a few moments, and check in with your throat area. How does it feel now? Is it different from before? In what way? How do you feel about speaking up to this person?

Allow yourself to let go of that scenario, and remember a time when you were happy while speaking to someone . . . Let your imagination help take you back to this experience, and begin to notice what happens in your throat . . . What thoughts or feelings accompany the sensations you are having? What is different about this situation than the previous one?

When you are ready, walk back through the doorway and come back into the room.

ART PROCESS: EXPLORING YOUR THROAT CHAKRA ENERGY

Go to your art materials, and create any part of your experience using whatever materials call to you.

WRITING

Using your non-dominant hand, dialogue with the image to find out more about this part of you.

II. SOUNDING EXERCISES

It is important that we begin to make sounds without purpose. The following three exercises allow the throat to open without having an agenda. There is no right or wrong sound you can make.

MATERIALS
Meditative instrumental music
The Spiral of Healing CD
Art materials
Journal or other writing notebook and pen

MOVEMENT

Begin with "Waking Up the Body." Once you have moved your body, continue with the directions.

1. Standing in a comfortable and relaxed position, begin by taking in a deep breath . . . On the out breath, allow yourself to make any sound you want, releasing energy and moving your body however it wants to move . . . Do this five times, slowly inhaling, stretching, or moving your arms out and up . . . When exhaling, allow any sound to come through . . . Breathe from your abdomen, not your throat, and notice the difference when you breathe out from your belly as opposed to when you breath from your throat . . . Notice the difference in the sounds . . . Again, allow for any movement that your body wants to make in association with the sounding.

2. Move your body, checking in with your sensations . . . Notice where in your body you feel tight or in pain, and breathe into that area, breathing out and sounding whatever it is you want to release from that particular area.

You can combine this sounding with a brief drawing of either the sounds you make or of the area in which you are focusing. Again, do not be concerned with the product or results, only the colors and movement on the paper and how it reflects your experience.

3. Check in with how you are feeling in your body . . . It may be a general sensation or a particular area that captures your attention . . . Briefly draw what you are sensing in your body, and after looking at the drawing, make sounds that reflect the drawing. First breathing fully in and on the out breath, make the sound that accompanies the drawing . . . There may be several different sounds for the different strokes you make on the paper . . . Sense each one and sound accordingly.

ART PROCESS: SOUNDING EXERCISES

In silence, create your experience of the sounding exercises with any material of your choosing.

WRITING

After each of the above sounding exercises, journal your experience.

III. GROUP SOUNDING

This is an exercise where you are authentically sounding and moving with yourself, listening to and responding to your own sounds while others are also moving and sounding around you. The sounds can be songs, gibberish, words, conversations, animal sounds, chants, or anything you want. This process encourages voice projection and trance states to release withheld sounds. It can be done with a group of two or more, depending on the size of the room. You will need enough floor space for movement so that no one moves into another person's space.

Use a timer, and the first time you do the group sounding, set the timer for fifteen minutes. With practice, the sounding portion of this process can go for as long as forty-five minutes.

MATERIALS
Meditative instrumental music
The Spiral of Healing CD

A bell, chimes, or instrument that makes a pleasant sound, or a timer
Art materials
Journal or other writing notebook and pen

MOVEMENT

1. After setting the timer, find a comfortable place in the room where you are not touching each other. Begin as a group to make sounds and move in any way that feels authentic as long as you do not bump into anyone else . . . You can also stand, sit, or lie down . . . The only guideline is to make continuous sound with eyes closed . . . This sound can be so quiet only the person sounding can hear it, or it can be loud so others hear and respond to it in their own movement or sounding . . . Continue to sound and move until you hear the timer.
2. Sounding Circle. The intention is to let go to your authentic sounding experience and travel with it. Everyone in the group lies in a circle with feet positioned toward the center but not touching each other. With experience, a group can lie with heads facing toward the center to experience less movement and more sound interaction. Begin with fifteen minutes. With practice, you can expand to one hour. This form lends itself to trance and to projection, so eyes are kept closed for the duration.

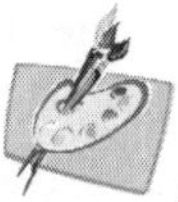

ART PROCESS: GROUP SOUNDING

In silence, create your experience of the sounding exercise with any material of your choosing.

WRITING

Journal your experience.

IV. YES/NO SOUNDING

The Yes/No exercise is an effective way to practice holding a position verbally and sensing it in the body. It can be done individually in front of a mirror and imagining the person to whom you are speaking, or in pairs with one person taking the "yes" stance and the other taking the "no" stance. Doing each part for several minutes and then trading positions is an effective way to feel the full impact of this exercise.

MATERIALS

Meditative instrumental music
The Spiral of Healing CD
Large mirror, preferably hanging or wall mirror
Art materials
Journal or other writing notebook and pen

MOVEMENT

Begin with "Waking Up the Body" (use CD or see page 59).

Take a centered stance in front of a mirror . . . Imagine someone you need to say no to . . . Begin to say "no" . . . Hear yourself say the word . . . Notice how your body changes when you say it . . . Try saying it in various tones—say it softly, then strongly, say it with joy, with anger, fear, and sadness . . . Each time you say it, stop afterward and check in with yourself . . . How does your body feel? How has your body responded to it? Are you convinced you mean it? Repeat it as many times as you need to until you believe yourself.

Next, say "yes" the same way, using various tones as you say it and checking in with yourself each time you say it . . . Notice the difference between saying "yes" in an angry way and in a fearful or joyous way . . . Say "yes" as many times as you need to until you are certain you believe yourself.

ART PROCESS: YES/NO SOUNDING

Use whatever materials move you as you image your experience of speaking these words. Try focusing on how you felt saying "yes" and image that. Then image the "no" experience. Let the art inform you further about your ability to stand by what you say and say what you mean.

WRITING

Journal about your experience. Which word was easier for you to say and mean when you said it, "yes" or "no"? How did your body respond to these words?

ADDITIONAL EXERCISES AND QUESTIONS

1. What were the communication patterns in your family when you were young? Did you feel heard? Were you encouraged to explore self-expression? What are your fears about speaking out? Do you say what you mean and mean what you say?
2. Write a letter to someone with whom you have unfinished communication. Tell the truth in the letter, saying everything you have always wanted to express. Do not mail it, but hold onto it. In one month, review the letter and notice how you feel when you read it again.
3. What are your favorite songs? What songs from childhood stay with you? How often do you sing or hum? What stops you from singing?
4. Spend at least five minutes each day singing. This can be in the car, along with the radio, in the shower, or anytime you feel like it. Notice how you feel after a week of singing, if this is new for you.

5. What projections are you aware of? In what stage are you with respect to these projections, and what are the qualities you need to integrate?
6. What is your definition of being "strong-willed"? Who has control over you, and whom do you control by your will?
7. How do you feel about surrendering your will to divine will? How do you sense guidance in your life, and do you trust it?

6.

MINDFUL VISION

SEEING WHAT WAS, WHAT IS, AND WHAT COULD BE
Brow (Sixth) Chakra

In the garden of gentle sanity,
May you be bombarded
by coconuts of wakefulness.
—Chogyam Trungpa Rinpoche

Focusing inward is a wonderful way to sooth the mind. Take a few moments now to do the following brief relaxation and centering exercise. First, read the next paragraph and then sit comfortably and allow yourself the reflection.

> Close your eyes and take three deep breaths through your nose, letting the air fill your belly slowly . . . With each in-breath, call in a quality you could use right now, like openness, love, or clarity . . . See that quality coming in on your breath as a color you like . . . Let the quality move through your body, bringing relaxation to your eyes, your chest, your belly—all parts of you . . . On each out-breath, release any thought that blocks your receiving this quality in this moment . . . Sense the movement as a gentle breeze drifting throughout your entire body, and feel the release in the same easy way . . . Appreciate your imagery; it helps you center yourself.
>
> Open your eyes, and continue reading.

There is an important relationship between our history, our experience now, and our dreams for the future. We try to be present, often thinking it means to the exclusion of anything past or future, yet we must realize that being present includes all that we are, all that we have grown through and lived through, and all of our future wishes. They are living together inside us. Sometimes it works in the negative in that our fears from the past and our future projections consume the present. We think that if only we were somewhere else—the magical "there"—we would be happy; we do not see that where we are now is the right place to be.

Consider the past and future as concepts and that life exists only in the moment. We might not like what is happening. We might want it to shift, but what if we could just hold the awareness that who we are and what we are doing in this moment is a composite of all we have lived through, all we bring into every moment, and all we hope for? Every experience we have had is always flowing through our imagination and is remembered in our body-mind.

We live in a culture that honors mind over matter. This translates into valuing thought over feeling or intellectual ideas over embodied knowing. The idea that matter or body is not as good as higher thought derives from an old Augustinian principle, that the flesh is sinful. Matthew Fox refutes St. Augustine in his book, "Sins of the Spirit, Blessings of the Flesh," where he states that the flesh of the human body and of the material world is a gift and a blessing. Our sins, he believes, begin with our inability to honor and bless the body, earth, and cosmos.[1] This is so true when we attempt to heal any physical, emotional, mental, or spiritual dis-ease.

There is a concrete relationship between a spiritual journey (striving for something better, creating happiness or feeling fulfilled) and the material plane (body and earth). We need a human body to feel and sense passion and joy. We live within the modern reality that splits mind from body and, at the same time, value diversity of thought and new ideas that welcome the body as sacred. Our minds and imaginations are tools. They are not the master. They are a servant just as our feelings serve us, but we cannot let them take over. We need to be in balance. When our minds and hearts are aligned, we can manifest anything we want. Our will has a clear path because we are not in conflict with ourselves.

Our minds need to be active and focused on something. When we do that, we calm down. This is one of the principles of meditation. It is important to still the mind and focus it on an inner reality, an inner sound, a vibration. The best use of our mind comes when it is in a still place. When we are underwater and we kick up the sand, it gets murky. After a while, it settles down, and then we can see and receive the beauty that lies in the ocean. This is like the mind. If we can let the mind calm down, we are given an expansive awareness that is beyond our present reality.

SIXTH CHAKRA AND DEVELOPING MATURING

The sixth chakra is traditionally known as the brow chakra, or the third eye, and is located in the center of the forehead where the eyebrows meet. All thought, imaginings, intuition, and ways of seeing emanate from this chakra. One of the most important endocrine glands, the pituitary, is found in this region. It is often called "the master gland" because it is responsible for secreting hormones that control the thyroid, sex organs, and the adrenals, as well as producing natural opiates that help the body reduce pain, stress and depression. This is one of the more obvious places to see the connection between mind and body, or thoughts, emotions, and body processes. Developmentally, the sixth chakra is a place of maturity and purpose. Here, we reclaim the right to see what was, what is, and what can be. It is about growing one's insight and mental capacities to know a greater truth without blaming or judging others and to free ourselves from patterns of denial. With the ability to see or sense a situation beyond a narrow frame of reference, we can expand our consciousness and grasp realities heretofore unavailable to us. We learn to see the bigger picture, to gain a greater perspective and to come out of one's personal story to a collective experience. This is the blossoming of wisdom.

Many spiritual traditions offer meditation as a means of first stilling the mind to allow for an experience of transcendence or expanding consciousness that supports our intention and ability to step back and perceive life differently. It is through the daily practice of being in silence that we drop into the present moment and experience what is. Sometimes, it is difficult or painful to acknowledge what is, but if we have the intention to feel it and let it go, experiencing the Via Negativa, we can use our creative will to bring ourselves back into a greater awareness of the moment. This is often referred to as coming home.

Another support we have is our capacity for dreaming, both night and day dreams. When we pay attention to what is coming to us in our dream life and decipher the symbols, we are often led to our life purpose or dream, which we may have carried since childhood. When we allow our thoughts to soften in our daydreaming by switching from a rational state to a relaxed altered state, we can also expand our awareness and become present to ourselves in a new way. This was the purpose of the guided visualization at the beginning of the chapter.

EMBODYING THE UNCONSCIOUS MIND

Our thoughts influence and shape our experience. If we carry pleasant thoughts, we usually have a pleasant experience. Likewise, when we obsess in negativity, we find ourselves in situations of pain.

In Western culture, the mind separates thought from feeling and relies on a linear way of viewing the world. For most of us this leaves out a considerable amount of perception like body language and sensations, imagery, feelings, nonrational knowing, and heartfelt communication. In order to heal, we need a totality of experience that involves not only the right and left hemispheres of the brain but our entire body.

"In the popular lexicon," notes Candace Pert, "connection between body and brain has been referred to as 'the power of the mind over the body.' But in light of my research . . . mind doesn't dominate body, it *becomes* body—body and mind are one . . . . The body is the actual outward manifestation, in physical space, of the mind . . . it is inseparable from the mind."[2] In this way, our body receives and stores all emotional experiences in the nervous system. The catharsis of illness may express the sudden, overwhelming release of information that has been trapped or repressed in the body. In this way, the body expresses the subconscious mind.

SPIRITUALITY AND INTELLIGENCE

The sixth chakra acts as the mental center of the body. Here, the interaction of the mind and psyche lead to intuition, insight, and wisdom. The challenges of working with the energies of this chakra include opening our minds to new thoughts and retrieving our power from where we have lost it in believing false truths. We have the opportunity to act on internal direction and discriminate between fear and danger. We are also challenged to separate truth from illusion and to use detachment when we can to give us a broader perspective.

Carolyn Myss explains that, "Our mental energy body is a combination of what knowledge we possess, what we believe to be true, facts, fears, personal experience, and memories. We can get to wisdom through detachment, which is a state beyond personal mind."[3] Once we accept what is and acknowledge the power of our own thoughts, we can simply notice them but not act upon them. In this way, we detach from the energy of the thought.

Writer Harrison Owen has identified what he calls the Four Immutable Laws of the Spirit, four principles that can assist us on our journey.[4] These principles speak to the power of presence and ask us to meet the moment open and unattached to outcome. Implicit in these laws is trust.

The first principle is "Whoever is present are the right people to be there," and refers to the notion that we are in the right place at the right time and that there are no mistakes. The second principle is "Whenever we start is always the right time," and says that there is no hurry, that we are ready when we are ready. The third principle is "What happens is the only thing that could have happened," and reminds us to learn in every situation and to accept a larger guidance system than the one with which we are familiar. The fourth principle is "When it's over, it's over," and is the ultimate acceptance of endings and deaths, allowing for the cycle of new beginnings. It is a personal favorite of mine for letting go.

Another theme of the sixth chakra is creativity.[5] To balance this chakra, we need an active intellectual and intuitive life—the balance of the right and left brain. Our society may still be out of balance in its preference for thought over feeling, but it does not serve us to swing to the opposite pole (intuition only) and discount intellect (reason). It is best to retrieve our intuition and balance it with clear thinking. By accessing both aspects, we can develop and create a meaningful experience.

We are also best served by creating a new relationship between the adult rational part of ourselves and the playful, emotional, and irrational childlike qualities within us to activate the energizing state so necessary for creativity. By doing this, we recognize that the first and sixth chakras are connected through early core beliefs that get in our way as well as through the innocence, awe, and wonder of the child, which can lead to creativity and intuition. Angeles Arrien explains that "if we maintain our sense of humor, spontaneity, and childlike curiosity, we are able to creatively use . . . and trust our perceptions, insights, dreams, and visions.[6] Utilizing our creativity allows us to retrieve our own life dream or purpose. Our life dream, or mythos, is held in those childhood activities that we were drawn to. When we re-examine our early ideas and present longings, we often find they are more closely related than we may have imagined.

THE SIXTH CHAKRA AND HEALING

In reclaiming the ability to see what was and what is in order to heal past wounds, we look at early experiences and how core beliefs have been implanted in our psyche during childhood. If our needs were not met as children, we learned to adapt to this trauma by developing a meaning around why this happened. For instance, if we were abandoned, we might conclude that we were unlovable. If we were neglected, we might decide we were not worthy of attention. If we were constantly criticized or chastised, we might agree that we were not good or good enough. When pain and shame replace love, our thoughts become fear-based and constricted. We understandably stop venturing out to explore our world and ourselves and, instead, through thoughts and perceptions, create a very small but safe world within which to operate.

When we recall our history, we may face more than we may want to, but by confronting the truth of what happened, we have the opportunity to free ourselves from guilt over past early decisions and forgive our inability to rise above difficult situations. Seeing how these old beliefs gave rise to attitudes, feelings, and behaviors that are not true but affect us still helps us make new choices and gain the courage to journey outside the box we have created for ourselves. Reclaiming the right to see what was and what is gives birth to a vision of what can be, not only for ourselves but for all life around us. As the Spiral takes us more deeply into ourselves, it also propels us out of ourselves into the greater community, where we can make a difference.

THE SIXTH CHAKRA AND THE VISIONARY ARCHETYPE

Honoring our future dreams and visions is as important as honoring our early experience of life. Invoking the Visionary archetype allows us to look beyond the box to where our passion is waiting and make goals to fulfill them. The Visionary archetype invites us to speak truth without blame or judgment. This is how we can combine the energies of head and heart. When they work together, we can activate will and manifest anything. When they oppose each other, we cannot positively move forward. "Should" and "cannot" are two words that prohibit our heart from joining in, and we are caught in a whirlwind of thought and emotion. In this whirlwind, we get nowhere and manifest nothing.

We express the Visionary when we honor our intuition, perception, insight, and vision and when we honor the power of prayer. We also connect with this energy when we give voice to what we see internally and externally and when we bring forward our creative spirit and life dream. When we throw off the shrouds of insufficiency (our negative self-talk), we can properly don the jeweled robe of our gifts and talents waiting to be manifested. This is imaginative language for converting old core beliefs that keep us small and fearful into new thoughts and affirmations that help us realize our hopes and dreams.[7]

By connecting to our playful authenticity and revising the old personal and cultural perceptions that limit our possibilities, we act in accordance with visionary activism, a concept that Caroline Casey has explored in depth. Visionary activism invites us to participate actively in shaping and creating our personal and collective reality by embarking on an adventure of joyful self-cultivation. By activating our inner visionary, we can bring forth our passions and dreams in a time when they are sorely needed. In so doing, we can effect change in the world. Casey describes it this way:

> "The all-too-visible forces of greed are stupidly lumbering along, dragging everything in their net toward the abyss of planetary system collapse. But the forces of human ingenuity and artful compassion, allied with the world of the invisibles, are sprightlier, sleeker, and smarter, and they know how to dance away from the chasm.
>
> If imaginative people can use their powers to release creation from the net, then the forces of greed can hurtle themselves into the abyss (to be transformed at a later time) without taking the rest of us."[7]

Casey has identified seven principles of visionary activism that guide our way in learning to manifest our personal and collective reality.[8] The foundation for the seven principles is the "zero principle," where we are invited to "believe nothing, but entertain possibilities." This means we can listen to something new without having to accept or reject the idea being presented. We are free to sense it without any commitment.

> Principle 1. *Imagination lays the tracks for the reality train to follow.* Here, we are encouraged to see that all that we are is the result of what we have thought. We have the power within us through our imagination to create what we want. The cultivation of imaginative capacity is an act of magic and mystery. We do not need more power, magic, or wealth. We need only to use the abundance we already

possess in conscious, imaginative ways. This allows us to be able to own our creative life force and to use it.

Principle 2. *Better to create prophesy than to live prediction.* What makes us passive (prediction) is toxic. What makes us active is tonic (prophesy), the cocreation with the divine.

Principle 3. *The invisible world would like to help, but spiritual etiquette requires that we ask.* Here, we are invited to understand that while help is always available, we need to open ourselves, drop our pride, and ask. We are not supposed to live our lives alone. We are always in community. There is not one aspect of creation that works independently. No plant or cell lives outside of community. This notion speaks to our need to make effort, to ask for what we need, and to have faith that we are not alone.

Principle 4. *The only way the gods know we're asking for help is ritual.* Casey offers a way to contact the invisible world. Ritual is any physical act, be it mundane or theatrical, that we imbue with invisible intention.

Principle 5. *If something's a problem, make it bigger.* Here Casey addresses our need to transform in order to manifest. Get obsessed, but do it ritualistically. Allow for full expression of the problem to experience its solution.

Principle 6. *We only possess the power of an insight when we give it expression.* This principle speaks to our need for creative energy. By bringing our creative life force to bear, we can utilize the power of our sixth chakra and share our creativity with others.

Principle 7. *Creativity comes from the wedding of paradox. We aspire to be disciplined wild people who are radical traditionalists.* Casey is asking us to think outside the box and to bring the sense of duality or opposition together in a creative and forward moving way.

These principles help us participate in the cocreation of our reality and invite us to be present and face our challenges with power and assistance. Just to remember that we can entertain new ideas but never have to believe them allows our bodies and minds to relax in the face of thoughts that may challenge the perceptions and beliefs we were raised to observe. Realizing that we are not alone in our journey and that help is waiting for us to reach for is very comforting.

Seeing what was, what is, and what could be helps us focus and organize our lives. Embodying the information that we have gained helps us to receive spiritual direction that we can put to use on the physical plane. This is the role of the ruler within, whom you will meet in the next chapter. The creative processes that follow will help you connect the left and right brain and will lead you, hopefully, to mindful vision.

CREATIVE PROCESSES

I. CORE BELIEFS

In this process, you are invited to bring together the energy of first chakra with the thought processes of the sixth. From your early experiences, you developed core beliefs as strategies for surviving difficult experiences. Here, you are invited to get in touch with the thought or idea that you continue to carry and listen to in your present life.

MATERIALS

Meditative instrumental music
The Spiral of Healing CD
Art materials
Journal or other writing notebook and pen

MOVEMENT

Begin with "Waking Up the Body" (use CD or see page 59). As before, gently move, breathing and focusing momentarily on each part as you travel up your body to the top of your head. Return to the throat area, focusing on the area from your ears to the top of your shoulders. Notice any sensations, emotions, or thoughts as you pay attention to this area. Relax your jaw and neck. Get comfortable either sitting, reclining, or standing.

GUIDED VISUALIZATION

Remember a time when you were having fun or doing something you loved to do as a child. What do you see yourself doing? Was there something that you wanted to do as a child but never let yourself do? What beliefs kept you from doing it? Imagine yourself doing the desired activity, and sense your body as you imagine it . . . Are you outdoors or inside? Are you engaging your body? How did you feel in your body? Do you engage in this activity today?

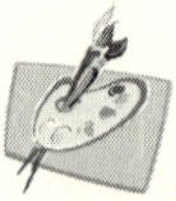

ART PROCESS: CORE BELIEFS

Image your experience using whatever art materials call to you.

WRITING

Journal about your experience.

II. VISUAL THINKING

In this art process, we focus on that aspect of presence that is historical. We actively bring forth into present time a situation from the past that is still having an effect on you today.

MATERIALS

Meditative instrumental music

The Spiral of Healing CD

Art materials, including four pieces of white paper, oil or chalk pastels or colored marking pens

Journal or other writing notebook and pen

MOVEMENT

Start with "waking up your body" (CD or page 59), keeping your attention within your breath and body. Then get comfortable, and begin the visualization.

GUIDED VISUALIZATION

Begin by bringing your attention to your belly. Sense or feel your belly breathing . . . Sense it going out and coming in . . . Sense your liver and the organs in your solar plexus breathing . . . Feel your liver taking in air and letting it go . . . Sense your heart breathing, feel the rhythm breathing in and out . . . Drop to your hips and legs, and sense these areas breathing, taking in air and letting it out . . . Drop to your feet, toes, the balls and soles of your feet, and sense your feet breathing in and breathing out . . . Come up into the palms of your hands, and sense them breathing in and breathing out. Feel the energy move between your hands . . . Come up into your jaw and mouth, and feel your mouth breathing . . . Come up into your eyes and forehead to the space between your eyes where the pituitary gland is and your "third eye." Sense or imagine your third eye breathing, taking in, distributing, and releasing.

Recall a time, a thought, a person, an issue, or a situation that is affecting you today . . . It might be an old core belief. It might be a thought you learned in childhood, like "I'm not enough unless . . ." Maybe it is a relationship with someone, a family member, friend, or mate, or a work relationship you are struggling with. Call that image to mind . . . Maybe it is an emotional situation, like you can't understand why you can't get angry, or you always get angry, or why it is hard for you to feel joy or sadness . . . Or maybe it is a spiritual thought or concept that is bothering you, like "If I could still my mind, I'd be enlightened" or "I don't know why I feel disconnected from myself or others." Take a few moments to find one issue that stands out in your life right now . . . Notice how your body responds to this thought . . . Do you feel constricted anywhere? Does your breathing become shallow? More quickly? Do you go numb? Do you fly away, get foggy or spacey? Notice what is happening . . .

For contrast, think of something that is working in your life, something that is going well that feels good to think of . . . Maybe it is being aware of your progress or a compliment you've been given or an awareness of a strength . . . Notice how your body responds to that thought . . . Notice what happens to your breath, your shoulders, and other areas of your body . . .

Notice the difference between a positive thought and a difficult or challenging thought . . . How does your body show you the difference?

Our body is our teacher, our guide. When we move to the art process, become aware of what your body says to you when you go through different experiences and how it speaks to you . . . Does it tighten or loosen up? Does your breath deepen or go shallow? Are there places where you space out or go numb?

ART PROCESS: VISUAL THINKING

Take about fifteen minutes for each drawing. At the end of each drawing, give the piece a title.

1. On the first piece of paper, draw the situation. This is the issue that you have been thinking about visually.
2. Next, draw your worst fear about the issue. Pay attention to the sensations in your body as you do this piece.
3. On the third sheet of paper, draw your highest hope about the situation. Notice your body response.
4. Last, ask yourself, "In response to the situation, *what if*?" Draw an image that expresses the question "what if." You determine what this means. Check in with your body.

WRITING

Journal about the entire process.

III. CONSCIOUS PRAYER—AN EXERCISE IN VISIONING

This is an exercise in visioning and clarifying what you want in your life. The Conscious Prayer[9] is an opportunity to focus on a single, specific goal and bring forth the energies necessary to facilitate its manifestation.

MATERIALS

Journal or other writing notebook and pen

Art materials, including photographs for collage, and glue

WRITING

Your conscious prayer is your intention for what you want. This process is best used when you want to manifest something in your life.

What you're stating should be *S*pecific, *M*easurable, *A*ttainable, *R*ealistic, and *Ti*me-driven (SMART).

Be *specific* with the feelings and actions you want to manifest. Keep the sentences clear and focused.

1. Make sure that within the prayer, there is a way for you to *measure* or document what you are asking for. How will you know when you have received it?
2. Make sure that what you ask for in the prayer is *attainable* or truly viable for you. Can you achieve what you ask for?
3. In whatever you ask for, be sure it is *realistic* for you in terms of your greater self and your spiritual path.
4. Finally, break down what you want into practical, reasonable pieces so you can meet and sustain your goals in a *timely* manner.

There are six parts to this process.

1. Specific Goal. State in a sentence or two your specific goal and how you want to *feel*. For instance, if you want a partner, how would you likely feel if you had this partner? You might feel loved, excited, joyous, energized, secure, challenged to grow, content. *That* is what you truly want; that is being specific. You would therefore state the prayer: "I want to feel love, excitement, joy, energy, security, the challenge to grow, and contentment as a result of having a partner."
2. Recognition. Describe your concept of God or Spirit, Higher Power or Greater Intelligence. How do you experience divinity in your life? Write two sentences about this using the form in the following example:

"God is unconditional love. God is all-knowing and all-powerful. God is pure light."

3. Unification. This step in your conscious prayer acknowledges that you and your concept of Divinity are one. Everywhere you have written your word for divinity, write it in this next section, replacing that word with the word "I." For example, where you may have written "God is unconditional love," you would write it the second time as "I am unconditional love." "God is pure light" would be written the second time as "I am pure light."
4. Realization. Knowing the truth about yourself, that you and Divinity are one, you know you can have what you ask for. Go back to what you stated in Part One. Where you have said you want something, write it now beginning with these words: "Knowing the truth about myself, that Divinity and I are one, I *am* lovable, excited, joyous, energized, secure, challenged to grow, content." In this example of desiring a partner, you could add: "I draw toward me like people, and I have the potential for partnership in my life."
5. Gratitude. Here, state what you are thankful for, including the sacred truths in life that help you get what you want. Write as much as you want expressing gratitude. This is an important part of the process.
6. Release. In this final part of the prayer, you are literally releasing the words of the conscious prayer to the divine, knowing that it is already handled. An example would be: "I lovingly release this prayer to the Spirit, knowing that my thoughts are received and accepted, and all that I speak is true." End with words that are a part of your tradition in prayer, like "Amen" or "Blessed be."

When you have finished the writing, type or neatly write up the full prayer.

ART PROCESS: CONSCIOUS PRAYER—AN EXERCISE IN VISIONING

Create a meaningful collage or other piece of artwork and attach the prayer to it. Hang this on the wall where you can read it every day.

ADDITIONAL EXERCISES AND QUESTIONS

1. Begin a daily practice of sitting in silence with yourself. If you do not have a particular practice, begin with visualizing your safe place and stay there until you feel calm and still. Then visualize a situation you want help with, and while staying in your safe place, allow an answer to emerge. Stay detached from a particular outcome, and allow any image, feeling, thought, or sensation to emerge. Take time to write your experiences down. Listen to your own wisdom.
2. Honor your dreams by recording them in a dream journal. Try to record and draw at least one dream per week.
3. Read your conscious prayer at least once a day, and notice any body sensations or reactions you have. Note them in your journal.
4. What activities did you love to do as a child that you have denied yourself as an adult? Remember a time when you were involved in those activities, feel it in your body, and commit to doing one of those activities this month.
5. What aspects of your past, present, or future do you have difficulty seeing? What belief supports your inability to see or vision for yourself? Journal about this.
6. What negative core beliefs continue to affect your life today? Write down your core beliefs—i.e., unworthiness, being unlovable. Which ones are you willing to re-examine and transform into new beliefs and affirmations? Try the visual thinking exercise in this chapter, and apply them to each belief. Allow yourself plenty of time to be with each belief. There is no hurry.
7. What is your relationship to detachment? In what situations are you detached, and in what situations are you attached to your position, way of thinking, or outcome? It is difficult to detach from something if you have never been attached or related to it. What do you think of this spiritual concept?

7.

AND THEN THERE WAS LIGHT

MYSTICISM AND THE EMBODIMENT OF SOVEREIGNTY
Crown (Seventh) Chakra

Can you lead your people
Without seeking to control?
Can you open and close the gates
In harmony with nature?
Can you be understanding
Without trying to be wise?
Can you create without possessiveness
Accomplish without taking credit, lead without ego?
This is the highest power.
—*Tao* [1]

From insight and vision in the brow, we travel to the crown of the head. Here, we continue to explore the expanded consciousness of our minds, where we discovered that what was, what is, and what can be are related. We can open to the realm of spirit, which comes through us in the form of our guides, or the Crone, the Sage, and all the wise ones within us.

How we get our knowingness and an actual embodied understanding of our place, our life purpose, and our relationship with the greater cosmos is a part of the realm of the seventh chakra. Known as the "thousand-petal lotus" in many spiritual traditions, this energy vortex links us to the cosmos and signifies wholeness and completeness. The seventh chakra also connects and relates to the universality of all people and thus to the building of community. It is about gathering one's light energy and fire from the other chakras and extending it into relationships with other light beings in the universe. As this happens, we connect with ancestors and family lineage. Community then cycles us back to first chakra and to our relationship to tribal energy. The difference between the first and the seventh is that what was once personal is now collective or symbolic.

The seventh chakra unites us to different realms and to an expanded consciousness. We are connected to and have an energetic relationship with what is above as well as below, connecting spirit with matter. When we talk about calling in ancestors and spirit guides to help us, we are talking about opening our seventh chakra and having an awareness of our connection to both Earth and Cosmos. We move away from smaller patterns of thought to embrace a deeper and broader point of view. We transcend the individual to a sense of oneness, peace, and understanding with all life, thus gaining a greater perspective and wisdom.

The seventh chakra is our connection to our spiritual nature and the vehicle for the embodiment of spirit. The crown is the entry point for the life force to enter the body, which pours in from a source beyond us called Universe, God, Love, Tao, or Great Spirit. This force nourishes our body, mind, and spirit and influences the nervous system, muscles, and skin. By focusing on this energy through prayer and various forms of meditation, we can develop a greater internal awareness of devotional, inspirational, and prophetic thoughts, ideas, and mystical connections. It also allows us the capacity for symbolic sight, spiritual vision, and intuition beyond ordinary consciousness.

Developmentally, we move through maturity into eldership as we enter the seventh chakra. The issue becomes one of surrender in that we must trust enough in the process of life to let go to a greater knowing. It allows us to live more fully in the present moment and to retrieve the right to have a greater perspective. It is also a time in our lives when we take our gifts and talents and give back to the community by sharing our wisdom and leaving a legacy. For this to happen, we must be aware of our life purpose or sacred path. It is the understanding and healing of past experiences and a reclamation of our strengths that provides us the fertile ground we need to bring forth these fruits of our labors.

Because we are working in the symbolic or spiritual realms, the seventh chakra opens us to an awareness of support that we may not have been aware we have. The use of imaginal process can help here, awakening our connection to guidance, which comes in many forms. There are many ways to experience guidance. The seventh chakra helps us find our unique and personal connection to it. Some people experience this guidance as intuition or gut reaction. Others relate to angels, spirit guides, and ancestors who surround them. Still others sense clarity where there once had been fog.

WALKING A SPIRITUAL PATH
THE DARK NIGHT OF THE SOUL

> Spirituality
> Is not to be learned by flight from the world,
> By running away from things,
> Or by turning solitary and going apart from the world.
> Rather, we must learn an inner solitude,
> Wherever or with whomsoever we may be.
> We must learn to penetrate things
> And find God there.
>
> —*Meister Eckhart* [2]

In our strength, developed through the processes that brought us here, we gain faith in divine guidance and trust our insights and "aha" experiences. We recognize synchronicities as the language of spirit, and we open to being "outside the box" in our thoughts and imaginings. When we allow ourselves to walk a spiritual path and seek union with divine energy, we are asking to have all our physical, psychological, and emotional illusions removed from our lives so we can recognize truth. Many inspirational texts of various traditions speak of this journey as the "dark night of the soul." This "dark night" often follows a spiritual crisis of some kind. We may think we are having an emotional problem or mental block, but often, what has been characterized as a psychological issue is really a spiritual emergency or the emergence of a spiritual reality that has not been fully integrated into our psyches.[2] This emergence often comes with a physical illness or trauma.

A spiritual crisis usually begins with an awareness of the absence of meaning or purpose that cannot be remedied by changing external aspects of our life. Something is trying to wake up inside, but we do not know how to see it. Strange new fears develop including the fear of losing touch with our sense of self or identity. We are no longer sure of what we want or who we are.

In a spiritual crisis, there is also a need to experience devotion to something greater than us, to be in contact with a sense of power that transcends human limits. We need to touch into miracles and hope.[3] We cannot fairly blame others for causing the crisis; the cause lies within and is most often a form of disconnection from our true nature. As we may know from experience, an unsatisfactory job, a "bad" relationship, or a particular health issue is often a consequence of the crisis and not the cause. Sometimes, illness can act as the catalyst for a spiritual transformation. When this happens, inspirational books can be good support, as can journaling about our experiences, praying, finding or continuing to follow a spiritual practice that nourishes us.

Another route to spiritual transformation at a time like this is to use our creativity to inform us and deepen our connection to our own guidance. This is the experience of the Via Negativa, the place of emptying and letting go. While it may sound, at first, negative, the Via Negativa is actually an opportunity. The Via Negativa can move us into the experience of cocreating our life with divinity. It is an important journey into the mystery. The benefits of this journey can increase when we use our creative energy: Being alone with our writing, drawing, singing, dancing, poetry, or silence can support our journey through our darkness into the light. If we still feel stuck, it may be helpful to work with a spiritually based therapist or counselor who can adequately hold the experience and bridge both the psychological and spiritual worlds to help ease our way into transformation.

Like all of creation, we are infused with divine, creative energy surging through us. Learning how to use it is part of the human journey and leads us to the experience of sovereignty. Working directly with the questions, feelings, and sensations that come from this "dark night" experience can open us up to an integration of wisdom and compassion for ourselves and others. Because we are being proactive, we can feel empowered to transform our beliefs and recognize our relationship with divine energy.

SOVEREIGNTY—THE RULER ARCHETYPE

> Every human person is an aristocrat,
> Every human person is noble and of royal blood.
> Who is more noble than someone who is born, on the one hand,
> From the highest and best that a creature possesses
> And who, on the other hand, is born
> From the intimate depths of the divine nature
> And the divine wilderness?
>
> —*Meister Eckhart* 4

As we have journeyed through the body, we have worked with various energies that have assisted us in reclaiming our authenticity. From the divine child to the warrior, healer, teacher, and visionary, we have accessed different characters in our inner cast of players. While there are many more to know and integrate, the most important is the archetype that stands between heaven and earth: the Ruler or the King/Queen. If we imagine that we can now access protection when we need it, creativity when we want it, the ability to see what we need and manifest it, then it becomes important to utilize that part of us that has the ability to take those actions. What is required is an organizing principle to steward the power for the good of the whole. For this energy, we turn to mythology and ancient stories of leadership.

The King and Queen in ancient times had three functions: to be the representative of the Divine on Earth, to bless the land and all who lived on it, and to steward the power of all those who served them. If the King was ailing, the land was often barren. If the rulers were loved and in turn honored their subjects, the kingdom prospered. If the King was a tyrant, there were great conflicts among the people and personal power became more important than collective health.

The goal of a healthy ruler is a harmonious and prosperous kingdom. The ruler is a symbol of wholeness and the achievement of the integration of the self. The archetype unifies the wisdom of youth and age, male and female, and ego and spirit, and allows us to manifest divine truth in physical reality. The gifts of this unity are sovereignty, competence, and the ability to respond to life.

The task of the Ruler archetype is to take full responsibility for life and to find ways to express authenticity in the world. The Ruler also creates harmony and peace among all its parts, working together under its leadership. It promotes order, peace, material prosperity, and abundance in an environment that allows each part to develop and work cooperatively. When the Ruler archetype is active, we feel at home in the physical world and in charge of ourselves. We know what we need and how to get it. We take responsibility for the ways our outer world mirrors our inner reality and the ways our individual life affects the community. As the Ruler pays attention to the entire kingdom and rules fairly, our parts are organized in a working whole. We can then claim our power for good and at the same time be aware of the shadow or the misuse of power.

The King and Queen do not create life as much as maintain and govern it. They are always thinking of the larger social good and do not simply satisfy ego needs. They accept their limitations as well as their gifts and, more importantly, they accept the limitations of this mortal human life. The individual of the king or queen is not as important as the position he or she holds. History has shown us that often when a king has died, it is proclaimed, "The King is dead, long live the King." This refers not to the personality but to the continuation of the role, which is essential for the health of the kingdom.

This is also true in our daily life. We need to function from our own sovereignty to stay balanced and functioning. As we work to reclaim this important energy of the Ruler, we must be aware of the inner and outer forms of this archetype. The domain of the inner realm concerns issues of the interior life—feelings, sensations, thoughts. The outer realm encompasses the manifestation of our inner reality in our everyday life. Both are needed and must work together for us to achieve integration and wholeness. An example in myths and stories is "The Handless Maiden,"[5] where the Queen is not complete until she journeys into the forest to find her earthy wholeness and grow back her hands. She is only reunited with the King after he leaves his kingdom to search for his individual earthbound wholeness. It is when the two are reunited that the kingdom is restored.

SHADOW RULER

When calling in the archetype of the Ruler, we must be awake to the misuse of power and other behaviors that signal the shadow. When we are controlling, rigid, tyrannical, or manipulative, we are caught in the grip of the shadow Ruler. When we feel selfish, vindictive, and prone to self-indulgence, we need to look at how we are disconnected from the power to order our lives.

Shadow kings and queens operate out of a scarcity mentality. They are not fully in touch with their own power but instead need to get it by overpowering others. The problem is not that they manifest too much power but too little. Instead of ordering the kingdom, they bring chaos through conflict. Instead of blessing the realm, they bring famine through their own rigidity and intolerance.

The task of claiming the healthy archetype of the Ruler is to take full responsibility for our life by seeking healing of wounds or areas of powerlessness that are reflected in scarcity in our outer life. When we learn to develop skills and create structures for manifesting our dreams in the world, we begin to think of others as well as ourselves and to find ways of expressing our deeper self in the world. When we do this, we gain sovereignty, responsibility, and competence and can create a sense of harmony in our life and with others. Reclaiming our sovereignty allows us to have greater compassion for others as well as for ourselves.

When we view life through a broader lens, we can better understand why we are living and find ways to bring our passions and pleasures in line with our purpose. We no longer judge situations by what we learned as children. We are able to stand back and experience the symbolic or archetypal influences inherent in our actions. We appreciate and listen to the voices of the child, the protector, the lover, the healer, the teacher, and the visionary from a place of compassionate detachment. We act only after we sit quietly with ourselves and allow a knowing to spring forth from the depth of our wisdom and guidance. This is another way of saying that by embodying our sovereignty, we let go of our "shroud of insufficiency" and don our "jeweled robe." In this way, we honor our connection to the Spirit and Mystery and find our place in the diversity of life.

CREATIVE PROCESSES

I. ANIMAL SPIRIT GUIDE

This process invites you to connect internally with a guide in the form of an animal of the air, ground, or water. It is another way to get in touch with your own instinctual nature. This animal spirit guide is available to help you any time you call it.

MATERIALS

Prerecorded visualization or *The Spiral of Healing* CD
CD player
Instrumental music
Art materials
Journal or other writing notebook and pen or pencil

MOVEMENT

Start with "waking up your body" (use CD or page 59), beginning at your feet and ending at the top of your head. Spend some time breathing into and feeling every part of your body.

GUIDED VISUALIZATION

Get into a comfortable position, seated or lying down, and allow your attention to take you to the top of your head . . . Imagine an opening, like a cone, flowing upwards. Notice any color, textures, or body sensation when you do this . . . Think about a situation or issue that you are working with, and ask for guidance with it.

Now imagine that a special animal is being drawn to you and you to it . . . Notice what kind of animal it is, whether it flies or walks, crawls or slithers . . . How does it approach you? Travel together, and the animal will show you sights you have never seen before, places it frequents and knows very well . . . Take your time . . . This animal has a specific gift for you, some wisdom or object that you need right now in your life to help you, perhaps in response to your pending issue . . . Notice what that gift is . . . Ask any question of your animal guide . . . Be open to hearing whatever response you receive . . . When you feel complete, ask the animal how you can contact it in the future if you need to . . . Gently bring yourself back into your space and become aware of your environment.

ART: ANIMAL SPIRIT GUIDE

Using whatever materials call to you, create a symbol of your animal guide and/or the gift you received.

WRITING

Journal about your experience.

II. EMBODYING THE RULER ARCHETYPE

This is the first of two processes that activate the feeling of sovereignty or authority within you. For this exercise, prerecord each of the five movement sections. Turn on the music for the section, and play the recorded instructions at the same time, moving to the music as the words describe. When each movement is finished, pause to journal about your experience with it. Continue in this way until you have completed all five movements.

MATERIALS

Instrumental music that reflects the five qualities of movement described below: flowing, staccato, chaotic, lyrical, stillness. Gabrielle Roth's "Endless Wave" (Audio Resources, page 224) is good, particularly the second cut, or use five separate appropriate music selections, recorded in the order to be used.
CD player
Prerecorded visualization or *The Spiral of Healing* CD

Journal or other writing notebook and pen or pencil
Art materials

MOVEMENT

Start with "waking up your body" (use CD or page 59), or use the first cut of Gabrielle Roth's "Endless Wave" for a variation. It is called "Body Parts." Then follow her Wave going through the five rhythms listed below or play similar rhythms.

1. Flowing (medium tempo, circular movements):
   You are the ruler of your kingdom . . . Feel that as you move around the room . . . Imagine you are wearing a robe, you are dressed as if for a procession, you're wearing a crown on your head . . . What does it feel like to be in your royal personhood? Notice how you breathe as this being, notice how you move, what parts of you move . . . Is it easy, stiff, full, narrow? Be with your movement, calling in that organizing principle, the one that blesses the kingdom, honors, stewards the power, has complete responsibility for the balance and harmony of your kingdom . . . What colors surround you, delight you? What textures and shapes belong in your world? What do you notice around you as you walk through the space of your kingdom? What is the general feeling of your kingdom? Is it fast, slow, sultry, energetic, or easy? Notice how you feel as you move through your life as the royal personhood that you are . . . Feel the queenly part of you, the powerfully feminine part of you, the flowing aspect of this part of who you are . . . Bless those aspects and qualities, honoring all that is you.

2. Staccato or angular (steady drum beat):
   Let the beat guide you as you feel and express the lines and edges . . . There are no curves here; it is not circular anymore . . . Feel the sharp corners, the ninety-degree angles . . . In this kingdom, there are boundaries, markings, directions, lines . . . Feel these in your body as you move them . . . What is the most important rule or law in your kingdom upon which everything else rests? If you could have it any way you want—and you are, in fact, the ruler of your kingdom—what rule or law is it that governs you? If there is a rule you have been living by,

who put that rule into effect? Is it still important to have? Change what you do not want as you create the kingdom that works for you now . . . Feel free to use the floor space, moving your body on all levels.

3. Chaos (strong rhythmic drum beat):
   Bring together the angular and circular, the lines and the flowing beauty as you sense yourself moving in space, integrating the flow and the angles . . . See how they move together . . . It is much more natural than separating them . . . When you bring two energies together, two forces that are seemingly different join together . . . Out of this chaos, something new will be birthed . . . Remember to breathe and to keep your energy grounded as you move chaotically, in whatever manner that means to you right now . . . What has been chaotic in your kingdom? What are you ready to let go of? What could use some blessing? Throw it into the chaotic movement . . . Bless it as you let it go . . . Send it on its way . . . It has served you long enough . . . It no longer serves the entire kingdom . . . It is time to release it . . . Let it go from all parts of your body.

4. Lyrical (light, springy music):
   Out of chaos, something joyous and lyrical is born. You are transforming, lightening up . . . Feel what your life is now . . . Skip through your life in joyous awareness that you are in charge of your life, you have sovereignty over your life . . . You can, with help, remove that which no longer serves you and bring in what does . . . Feel the power of that, the knowingness, the energy of it . . . This does not mean it is easy, and you may need a lot of help, but you can do it . . . Move your body so you feel this awareness of your ability to let go, and prepare to be reborn into what you want . . . This is the dance of maturity, standing in who you are, holding all of you, feeling all of you, moving all of you . . . Blessing all of you.

5. Stillness (mellow, slow beat):
   This is the opportunity to come into yourself in an inward way. Move slowly and hold in stillness, or continue to move slowly and fluidly . . . Imagine that crown upon your head or the throne behind you . . . Feel the serenity and calm that comes from bringing together all that you need in harmony and balance. Drink it in, breathe it in . . . Feel your

center. Feel that which you stand upon as you bless this kingdom, as you take responsibility in the most respectful and loving way to receive the Spirit into you . . . Here, you own your participation in divinity, in the creative process of life, you move it out to manifest and share it, to create with it . . . Sense the energy coming in through the top of your head . . . It is like you are standing under a wondrous waterfall of light that is filling every cell of your being . . . As you take hold of your staff, chalice, or magic wand—your symbol of this position—see your different parts come before you so you can bless them . . . Honor the little ones for their energy, their creativity, their innocence and determination, their wild nature . . . Bless the hard workers, the ones who, no matter what, keep on going—the healers, the warriors, even the controllers . . . Bless them for the part they play . . . Bless the seekers and the lovers, the caretakers, the orphans and the destroyers, the ones who help you let go of what you no longer need . . . Bless the magicians and the sages and the fools that keep you light, that remind you that nothing is that serious except your openness and playfulness to life . . . Recognize their contributions to the whole of your kingdom, even the shadowy parts . . . Everything and everyone has a part to play.

ART: EMBODYING THE RULER ARCHETYPE

Using whatever materials call to you, capture in art the feeling you had in the movement of your Ruler. Create a symbol for your Ruler (crown, staff, or jeweled robe) that will remind you of your embodied experience.

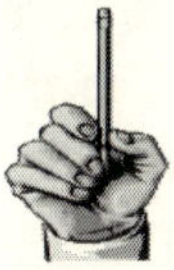

WRITING

Journal about the whole experience of embodying your Ruler.

III. MANIFESTING YOUR INNER RULER—THE FACE OF SOVEREIGNTY

This is an opportunity to create an outward picture of your inward experience of the royal personhood within you. It is the essential energy of your sovereignty in a mask that you can wear. By doing so, you can embody more fully the qualities of your Inner Ruler.

MATERIALS

Prerecorded visualization or *The Spiral of Healing* CD
CD player
Instrumental music
Art materials

GUIDED VISUALIZATION

Let your body be as comfortable as it can . . . Slowly take in three cleansing breaths, breathing in deep relaxation and breathing out the release of anything that interferes with your journeying deep inside yourself.

Imagine a community somewhere, perhaps in ancient times, perhaps more recent . . . In this community, village, or kingdom, you are deeply connected with the Earth and all of its creatures . . . As you wander through your community, notice the new plants growing . . . Recognize those good for eating and those good for medicines . . . Notice all the animals that support you and your loved ones, and give them blessing and gratitude for their sacrifice so you may live . . . You walk in harmony with nature, with the elements, and the Earth.

You are a respected elder who, along with others, governs wisely and fairly . . . As you move through your community, you are aware of your position and your responsibility . . . You feel honored to be of service to the Spirit as you are to the Earth . . . With your help, the community is ordered and functions well.

As you feel this presence within you, notice what textures and colors seem to reflect who you are . . . What do you look like? What symbols of your station do you wear? How does it feel to be in harmony with all things and to have the responsibility to order and bless the kingdom? Take as much time as you need to feel this.

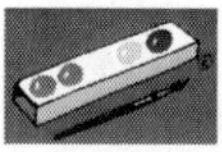

ART: MANIFESTING YOUR INNER RULER—THE FACE OF SOVEREIGNTY

When you are ready, create and decorate a mask to represent this important part of yourself. There are several ways to make a mask using a paper plate as a template or cardboard or even a paper bag. For those who want a more sophisticated mask, try using plaster gauze over a mold. Most art supplies stores can give you instructions and supplies.

Begin with the blank mask that you are using. Remembering the visualization, begin to find materials that will help you to create the mask that represents your vision. Take as much time as you need so you can really bring this archetype to life. Create eyes (or small holes) and a mouth so you can see and speak through it. Create a way to wear it.

WRITING

Journal about your experience making the mask. Here are some questions to ask your mask:

1. Where and when were you born?
2. What do you see in front of you?
3. How do I recognize you in my life, in my body?
4. What do you know that I need to know at this time?
5. Where are you living in my body?
6. How have you come to exist in me?
7. Tell me about yourself.
8. Ask the mask to respond to a specific question or issue you might have.

ADDITIONAL EXERCISES AND QUESTIONS

1. Do you have a spiritual practice? If so, what is it? How does it support your experience of compassionate detachment? If not, what stops you from engaging in such a practice? What ways do you bring yourself to a greater perspective of life?
2. What religious practices did you grow up with? How have these affected your relationship to Spirit?
3. Everyone has wisdom. In what areas of your life do you feel wise? How did you acquire that wisdom? If you could gain more wisdom in certain aspects of your life, what would these be and how would your life be different?
4. How do you experience guidance?
5. Have you ever had a spiritual crisis or spiritual emergence? What have you learned from this important experience?
6. How are you in touch with your Ruler archetype? What great lessons have you learned about your need for sovereignty?

8.

COMING FULL CIRCLE

INTEGRATING BODY, MIND, AND SPIRIT

Be content with what you have.
Rejoice in the way things are.
When you realize there is nothing lacking,
The whole world belongs to you.
—*Tao-Te-Ching* [1]

The Spiral of Healing is a process of discovery. Through words, movement, and creative art processes, you have discovered how each of your chakras holds both wounding and healing. You have discovered how resources such as strengthening tools like good boundaries, support, archetypal energies, and faith help support the healing of trauma that has been stored in your cellular tissue. And you have created a new relationship with your body by paying attention to and exploring without judgment what you sense. You have learned that your thoughts, emotions, physiology, and spirituality are in relationship with each other, and you can focus on integrating this vital information into your everyday lives.

THE INTERCONNECTING SYSTEM OF CHAKRAS

As you have discovered, the chakras do not work independently of each other; they are part of an overall energy system. Each chakra points to a developmental stage or life issue, a sacred truth or right to reclaim or a particular archetype that can be activated. Together, they act as a map to follow as we grow and heal.

Thoughts, emotions, body, creativity, and spirit interact to support the full use of energy in your chakras. The chakras below the heart have connections with those above, and both issues and healing reside in and throughout the body. For example, look at a challenging relationship which may be affected by early trauma (second chakra). In response, you can express yourself and use your will to reclaim your creative responses (fifth). If you are struggling to take charge of your life and the fear of abandonment (first, third) emerges, you can review your core beliefs, envision a new way to hold the old information, and be open to new support (sixth). In each case, you can understand how the body works together with mind and spirit to create wholeness and balance.

Another aspect of integration is noticing the movement of energy, which can be transformative. For example, you may feel stuck in one aspect of your life like finding work that fulfills you. As you gain skills and build your resources (discover what brings you passion and joy), you gain a wider perspective (and feel more confident to go after a job that fulfills), and the stuck energy is released. It's like a log burning; the wood becomes smoke, matter changes with the transformation, and energy is released. Movement of energy can also transform inspiration or guidance into matter. The inventor creates a new product; the sculptor molds a new form.

Whether you are manifesting or releasing energy, it is the whole system working together that creates the outcome. What happens when you want to create work you love and you are blocked by either an old belief that says that you are not worthy of happiness or by a fear that you are not good enough to be successful? You will have a wonderful idea and will be able to vision it, but when it comes to making it real, you will be stopped by those beliefs and embodied traumas that inhibit your ability to find options. Or maybe you are in an unhealthy relationship and feel trapped. You want to leave but are frozen by your fear of being alone and the inability to support yourself. Letting go of unhealthy situations requires a huge leap of faith in yourself and in the universe to support you. When you look at the flow of energy, you can see where in the chakra system you need to work so that movement can begin to happen.

As you sense the energy in your chakras, you may notice that while some feel full and flowing, others are blocked and small. Some of you may be very connected to your spiritual life yet unable to support yourselves or create loving relationships. Others may be very practical and function well in the world yet are unable to trust people and feel love and compassion. Your early coping strategies may either help or hinder you, depending on the reasons why you do what we do. Again, the answer is to look at the connections between the lower and upper chakras in order to gain more understanding.

What still affects you from your history usually controls your relationship to the world. If you value security above passion because you did not get your needs met as a child, you may find steady, reliable work that physically supports you but may inhibit your joy. If you value intensity above safety, you will take risks without much thought of the outcome. You may enjoy the rush of life, but you may struggle with the mundane activities that support your well-being.

INTEGRATING ARCHETYPAL ENERGY

To resolve imbalance in your chakras, you have learned that you can look to archetypes for help and reclaim lost or underdeveloped parts of yourself. When we do this, you feel more balanced and comfortable in our own skin. For example, you may find you are allowing your child archetypes to have all the power. This gives you great energy but little follow-through. Or you may be attending to the hurt child within, which needs a sense of safety at the expense of excitement. If your warrior is serving the child, you may be continuing old survival patterns that are no longer appropriate. You may find your caregiver is only giving to others instead of balancing it by meeting your own needs as well. You may find you are playing the shadow ruler, misusing your power with others or with yourself; doing this, you will never feel your own sovereignty and have compassion. Chances are, you will feel controlled by others, struggle to stand in your power, and fail to manifest a balanced and harmonious life.

Finally, it is helpful to consider how each chakra supports your healing. How have you been supported by the emergence of archetypal energies found in each chakra? How do you use this new understanding in your everyday life? Take a moment to get quiet with yourself, and listen for the answers to these questions.

CREATIVE PROCESSES

I. A FINAL SELF-PORTRAIT

Here you end where you began, completing the spiral experience in the art processes. This is an opportunity to image how you feel now, having completed the art processes and writing directives. Feel the integration of what you have learned. As you complete this new self-portrait, integrate the feeling of the archetypes to which you have been introduced as well as the awareness of your blocks and breakthroughs. Try using new materials. For example, you might create three-dimensionally or use collage if you drew before.

MATERIALS
Meditative instrumental music
The Spiral of Healing CD
Art materials
Journal or other writing notebook and pen

MOVEMENT/VISUALIZATION
Turn on the music and begin by moving to its rhythms . . . Allow yourself to feel your energy move as you sway and gently begin to move your body . . . Bring your awareness to your feet, ankles, shins, and knees, and move up your body until you have slowly moved every part of it that you can, including your jaw and eyes . . . Spend up to about five minutes with this.

Find your center by going off balance . . . rest your weight on one foot and then the other, tip forward and back, and gently rock back and forth and side to side until you sense an inner point of balance . . . Take a few minutes to do this.

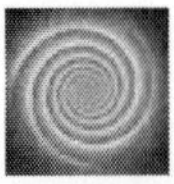

GUIDED VISUALIZATION

Check in with yourself . . . Sense what is moving through you, where you feel tight or loose, tired or energized . . . Ask yourself: What does my life feel like right now? How do I see myself? How do I feel about myself? When you are ready, go on with the art process.

ART PROCESS: A FINAL SELF-PORTRAIT

As with all of the art processes in this book, focus on your process, not on the product. Using whatever materials seem most descriptive of how you feel right now, create an image of yourself. Your self-portrait can be abstract or realistic and can include physical, emotional, mental, and spiritual aspects. Allow as much time as you need for this.

WRITING

To start, compare your new self-portrait with your original one and notice what is different. How have your understanding and awareness of your body and your experiences in creative process impacted the way you see yourself now?

Next, dialog with the image in your journal or on separate large sheets of blank paper. Using your dominant hand, welcome the image and ask it why it has come or what it is about (even if you think you know). You'll "hear" the answers in your imagination as you write them with your non-dominant hand. They may come in incomplete sentences and may not even make sense. Just keep with the process until there is some resolution or you wish to stop. Remember that imagery is a gift from your unconscious self and can open up doorways into building a healthy relationship between your mind and your body. If you like, read the dialogue aloud and write it into your journal if you have not already written it there.

Journal the following questions:

1. What do I see when I look at this image? Try not to jump to interpretations but see the image itself.
2. How do I feel about this image?
3. What is missing from this image?
4. What would I change in this image if I could?
5. What does the image tell me about myself?

9.

Epilogue

Sacred Unity: An Idea Becomes a Reality

Plant, so that your own heart will grow.
Love, so God will think,
"Ahhh, I got kin in that body!
I should start inviting that soul over for coffee and rolls."
Sing, because this is a food our starving world needs.
Laugh, because that is the purest sound.
—Hafiz[1]

When we recognize our inherent ability to become ourselves, we can see our strengths and challenges as learning opportunities instead of getting caught in the struggles of life. We can add tools and resources that support our emerging selves and work with our imagination to deepen our healing experiences. We can recognize that both light and dark lead to creativity and transformation and honor all our experiences as part of the journey. We can also recognize the fundamental relationship between mind, body, and spirit and between ourselves and all life forms. It is only in acknowledging our interconnectedness with creation that we can let go of separation and loss and embrace joy, compassion, and the hard work ahead to heal the planet.

The healing journey represented in this book begins with a personal, introspective focus through which we learn to develop courage, awareness, and strength. As this happens, we naturally seek to empower others and all forms of life, recognizing our cosmic interdependence. Out of one's healing comes the desire to serve and the means by which we can. That small focus then widens exponentially to include family, community, and, finally, the global interspecies collective of which all are a part. It is that longing for this communion that propels anyone to walk *The Spiral of Healing*.

It is difficult to get to the community level of service without first doing personal work. Once we have done that, we will have the available energy we need. Our chakras will be open, our energy will be flowing, and we will have gathered the tools by which to handle the challenges of life that come. In the same way, consciousness—living in a state of reality—begins personally and then expands to the community. So I speak of moving from a relative, or projected reality, to a truth without limit.

I have attempted to provide a way for any of us to discover and accept body, mind, and spirit so that we can retrieve enough of ourselves to be at choice, gain confidence, and have compassion for self and others. If this book has helped even one person to do this, then its purpose and mine have been fulfilled. Blessings and peace!

NOTES

Part I
Waking Up to Yourself: Creativity, Imagination, and Body Wisdom

1. Matthew Fox, *Creativity: Where the Divine and Human Meet* (New York: Tarcher/Putnam, 2002), p. 4.
2. Thomas Hanna, *Somatics* (Menlo Park, Calif.: Addison-Wesley Pub., 1998).
3. Candace Pert, "Your Body Is Your Subconscious Mind" (Denver, Colo.: Sounds True Recording, 2004).
4. Shaun McNiff, *Art as Medicine: Creating a Therapy of the Imagination* (Boston: Shambhala, 1992).
5. Matthew Fox, *Creativity: Where the Divine and Human Meet* (New York: Tarcher/Putnam, 2002).
6. Jeanne Achterberg, *Imagery in Healing: Shamanism and Modern Medicine* (Boston: Shambhala, 1985).
7. Meagan Pugh, "Somatic Art Therapy: Healing Body, Mind and Spirit," unpublished thesis (Sonoma State University, Rohnert Park, Calif., 1994).
8. Peter A.Levine and Ann Frederick, *Waking the Tiger* (Berkeley, Calif.: North Atlantic Books, 1997).
9. Matthew Fox, *Original Blessing* (Santa Fe, N.M.: Bear & Company, 1984).
10. Carolyn Myss, *Anatomy of the Spirit* (New York: Harmony/Random House, 1996), p. 79.
11. Candace Pert, *Molecules of Emotion* (New York: Scribner, 1997), pp. 142-143.
12. Anodea Judith and Selene Vega, *The Sevenfold Journey* (Freedom, Calif.: The Crossing Press,1993), pp. 17-19.
13. Carolyn Myss, *Anatomy of the Spirit* (New York: Harmony/Random House, 1996).

14. Matthew Fox, *Sins of the Spirit, Blessings of the Flesh* (New York: Harmony, 1995).

Help Is On the Way:
Reclaiming Resources and Strengthening Tools for the Journey

1. Peter Levine and Ann Frederick, *Waking the Tiger.* (Berkeley, Calif.: North Atlantic Books, 1997).
2. Angeles Arrien, *The Four-Fold Way* (San Francisco: Harper, 1990).
3. Brian Swimme and Thomas Berry, *The Universe Story* (New York: HarperCollins, 1992).
4. Peter Levine and Ann Frederick, *Waking the Tiger* (Berkeley, Calif.: North Atlantic Books, 1997).
5. Candace Pert. "Your Body Is Your Subconscious Mind," (Denver, Colo.: Sounds True Recording, 2004 CD)

Part II
Laying the Foundation:
Re-examining the Past, Retrieving the Healthy Child

1. Caroline Myss, Ph.D. *Sacred Contracts* (New York: Three Rivers Press, 2002), pp. 118-123.
2. Angeles Arrien, *The Four-Fold Way* (San Francisco: Harper, 1990).
3. Arrien, *Ibid.*
4. Carol Pearson, *Awakening the Heroes Within* (San Francisco: Harper, 1991).
5. Caroline Myss, Ph.D. *Anatomy of the Spirit* (New York: Harmony/ Random House, 1996), p. 79.

Entering the Fruitful Dark:
Finding Your Way with Creativity, Sexuality and Work

1. Ellyn Bader and Peter P. Pearson, *In Quest of the Mythical Mate: A Developmental Approach to Diagnosis and Treatment in Couples Therapy* (New York: Brunner/Mazel Publishers, Inc., 1988).
2. Oona Mourier and Jim Herriot, Ph.D., *9 Secrets to Bedroom Bliss: Exploring Sexual Archetypes to Reveal Your Lover's Passions and Discover What Turns You On* (Gloucester: Fairwinds Press, 2003), p.31.

3. Brian Swimme and Thomas Berry, *The Universe Story* (New York: HarperCollins, 1992).
4. Daniel C. Matt, *The Essential Kabbalah: The Heart of Jewish Mysticism* (San Francisco: Harper, 1995).
5. Charles Burack (Professor), University of Creation Spirituality, Oakland, California (Seminar: "Reinvention of Work," June 2000).
6. Matthew Fox, *The Reinvention of Work* (San Francisco: HarperCollins, 1995), p. 91.
7. *Ibid*, p. 114.

Take Me to My Leader: Discovering Identity and Personal Power

1. Caroline Myss, Ph.D. *Anatomy of the Spirit* (New York: Harmony/Random House, 1996), p. 179.
2. *Ibid*, pp. 185-192.
3. Angeles Arrien, *The Four-Fold Way* (San Francisco: Harper, 1990).
4. Matthew Fox, *One River, Many Wells* (New York: Tarcher/Putnam, 2000), p. 406.
5. *Ibid*, pp. 420-421.
6. Daniel Ladinsky, *The Gift: Poems by Hafiz, the Great Sufi Master* (New York: Penguin/Putnam, 1999)
7. Portia Nelson, *There's a Hole in My Sidewalk: The Romance of Self-Discovery* (New York: Atria Books/Beyond Words, 1994).
8. Wendell Berry, *Selected Poems of Wendell Berry* (Washington, D.C.: Counterpoint Press, 1998), "To Know the Dark," p. 68.
9. Angeles Arrien, *The Four-Fold Way* (San Francisco: Harper, 1990).
10. Matthew Fox, *Sins of the Spirit, Blessings of the Flesh* (New York: Harmony, 1995).
11. *Ibid*, p. 239.
12. Angeles Arrien, *The Four-Fold Way* (San Francisco: Harper, 1990), p. 41.

Home Is Where the Heart Is: Loving and Nurturing Self

1. Matthew Fox, *Sins of the Spirit, Blessings of the Flesh* (New York: Harmony, 1995), p. 107.

2. Otto Rank, *Art and Artist* (New York: Norton, 1932).
3. Matthew Fox, *Creativity: Where the Divine and Human Meet* (New York: Tarcher/Putnam, 2002), p. 170.
4. Angeles Arrien, *The Four-Fold Way* (San Francisco: Harper, 1990), pp. 65-68.
5. Matthew Fox, *Creativity: Where the Divine and Human Meet* (New York: Tarcher/Putnam, 2002), p. 18.
6. Diane Dreher, *The Tao of Personal Leadership* (New York: HarperCollins, 1996), p. 23.
7. Julia Cameron, *The Artist's Way* (New York: Tarcher/Putnam, 1992), quote by Agnes De Mille, p. 121.
8. Source unknown.

Speak Now or Forever Hold Your Piece:
Reclaiming Your Authentic Voice

1. Daniel Ladinsky, *The Gift: Poems by Hafiz, the Great Sufi Master* (New York: Penguin/Putnam, 1999), p. 281.
2. Angeles Arrien, *The Four-Fold Way* (San Francisco: Harper, 1990), p. 96-98.

Mindful Vision:
Seeing What Was, What Is, and What Could Be

1. Matthew Fox, *Sins of the Spirit, Blessings of the Flesh* (New York: Harmony, 1995).
2. Candace Pert, *Molecules of Emotion* (New York: Scribner, 1997), p.187.
3. Caroline Myss, *Anatomy of the Spirit* (New York: Harmony/Random House, 1996), p. 207.
4. Angeles Arrien, *The Four-Fold Way* (San Francisco: Harper, 1990), Harrison Owens, p. 112.
5. Matthew Fox, *Sins of the Spirit, Blessings of the Flesh* (New York: Harmony, 1995).
6. Angeles Arrien, *The Four-Fold Way* (San Francisco: Harper), 1990.
7. Caroline Casey, *Making the Gods Work for You* (New York: Harmony), 1998.
8. *Ibid*, p. 14.

9. This form of Conscious Prayer is inspired by the Center for Spiritual Living's "Spiritual Mind Treatment" process and was introduced to me in a personal communication by K. Noblin, M.F.T., in Santa Rosa, Calif., 1996. The Spiritual Mind Treatment is a form of prayer used by practitioners in healing rituals.

And Then There Was Light: Mysticism and the Embodiment of Sovereignty

1. Diane Dreher, *The Tao of Personal Leadership*, (New York: HarperCollins, 1996), p. 134.
2. Matthew Fox, *Meditations with Meister Eckhart* (Sante Fe, N.M.: Bear & Co., 1983), p. 90.
3. Stanislav and Christina Grof, *Spiritual Emergency: When Personal Transformation Becomes a Crisis* (Los Angeles: Tarcher), 1989.
4. Matthew Fox, *Meditations with Meister Eckhart* (Sante Fe, N.M.: Bear & Co., 1983), p. 94.
5. Clarissa Pinkola Estes, *Women Who Run with the Wolves* (New York: Ballantine, 1992), pp. 387-455.

Coming Full Circle: Integrating Body, Mind, and Spirit

1. Diane Dreher, *The Tao of Personal Leadership* (New York: HarperCollins, 1996).
2. Chakra meditation. Sources: reiki-for-holistic-health.com; healing.about.com; spiritualnetwork.net; iscali.co.uk; ewkerala.com; bellaonline.com.

Epilogue: Sacred Unity : An Idea Becomes a Reality

1. Daniel Ladinsky, *The Gift: Poems by Hafiz, the Great Sufi Master* (New York: Penguin/Putnam, 1999).

GLOSSARY OF TERMS

Activation	A heightened alert response in our sympathetic nervous system to some external or internalized experience which we register as dangerous.
Archetypal	Universal energy that resides with the unconscious psychological life of all people everywhere.
Archetype	A term that refers to the different aspects of our energy which we need to bring to consciousness. Among the specific archetypes referred to in this book are the Innocent, Orphan, Artist, Lover, Warrior, Healer, Teacher, Visionary, and the Ruler.
Autopoesis	A cosmic principle that speaks to the inner capacity within all life to participate directly in the endeavor of creation; it is our ability to become all that we are. For a more detailed description, see Swimme and Berry (1992).
Body-mind-Spirit	A term that refers to the connection between awareness and physical sensations that together produce a totality of human experience.
Chakra	A Sanskrit word meaning wheel or disk that is used to represent the spining vortices of energy in our body. Located within our nervous and endocrine systems, these vortices receive, assimilate and transmit life energy. The Chakra system is an ancient metaphysical diagram of the interrelationship between body, emotions, mind,

and spirit. For a more detailed description, see Judith (1993), Fox (1999), or Myss (1996).

Cosmogenesis A universal principal that refers to the ongoing evolutionary dynamics (the form producing powers) operating the same in every part of the universe. Cosmogenesis is characterized by differentiation, autopoesis, and communion. See Swimme and Berry (1992, p. 66-79).

Creation Spirituality A term that honors all of creation as an original blessing. Creation Spirituality integrates the wisdom of Western Spirituality and global indigenous cultures with the emerging post-modern scientific understanding of the universe and the awakening artistic passion for creativity which reveals the interrelatedness of all beings. The Creation Spirituality movement seeks to integrate the wisdom of western spirituality and global indigenous cultures with the emerging scientific understanding of the universe and the passionate creativity of art. See www.creationspirituality.org. or Fox 1984).

Four Paths of Creation Spirituality A four-fold journey that humans make to find their deep and true self. The four paths are:
Via Positiva: delight, awe, wonder, revelry;
Via Negativa: darkness, silence, suffering, letting go;
Via Creativa: birthing, creativity;
Via Transformativa: compassion, justice healing, celebration.

Defensive Orienting Responses These are the primary means through which we tune into our environment. The natural, programmed responses of our nervous system include expectancy, surprise, alertness, curiosity, and the ability to sense danger. They are forms of kinesthetic and perceptual awareness and are specifically the behaviors of fight, flight, or immobility or freeze. For more information, see Levine (1997) or Rothschild (2000).

Rapprochement A French word meaning the establishment of cordial relationships or reciprocity. In developmental terms, it means the stage when a young child is beginning her shift towards autonomy from symbiosis with the mother. In the in-between stage of rapprochement, a child needs the freedom to explore and the support to do it. For more information on this, see Bader and Peterson (1988).

Somatic Originated from the Latin word "soma" meaning "of the body" and refers to our awareness of ourselves from the inside out. Somatic refers to body-oriented conditions that combine consciousness and physicality.

Spiral Journey The natural movement of the journey of life. The path is spiral, circling around and coming back to itself while moving forward in time. As we do this, we are gathering tools and resources, meeting new challenges, and learning and growing through each cycle.

The Spiral of Healing

A training in Somatic Art Therapy created and facilitated by the author. Step-by-step creative arts and somatic processes that help someone heal by reclaiming a healthy relationship with one's body, mind, and spirit. It is a journey towards wholeness, through which one develops the courage, awareness, and strength to claim one's full humanity. On this journey, one gains faith in oneself and others, gather healing and strengthening tools, and forges a tangible working relationship with one's body.

Titration — The movement between the external force of trauma which ruptures the protective container of our experience and a counter or healing vortex to balance the force of the trauma vortex. This results in renegotiation of the trauma. Renegotiation is the overall process by which the traumatic response (constriction, hypervigilance, helplessness, and dissociation) transforms to natural vitality and aliveness.

Bibliography of Related Reading

Achterberg, Jeanne Imagery in Healing: Shamanism and Modern Medicine. Boston: Shambhala, 1985.

Angeles Arrien, *The Four-Fold Way: Walking the Paths of the Warrior, Teacher, Healer, and Visionary.* San Francisco, California: Harper, 1990.

______*The Second Half of Life: The Blossoming of Your Creative Self.* Audiotape Set, Denver, CO: Sounds True Recording, 1998.

Bader, Ellyn and Pearson, Peter P. *In Quest of the Mythical Mate, A Developmental Approach to Diagnosis and Treatment in Couples Therapy.* New York: Brunner/Mazel, 1988.

Berry, Wendell. *Selected Poems of Wendell Berry*. Washington, DC: Counterpoint Press, 1998.

Burack, Charles. Class Notes from "The Reinvention of Work," a seminar at the Doctor of Ministry Program at the University of Creation Spirituality, Oakland, CA, June, 2000.

Cameron, Julia. *The Artist's Way*. New York: Tarcher/Putnam, 1992.

Cappachione, Lucia. *Picture of health: Healing Your life With Art*. Carson, CA: Hay House, 1990.

Casey, Carolyn W. *Making the Gods Work For You*. New York: Harmony Books, 1998.

Chodron, Pema. *The Places That Scare You.* Boston: Shambhala, 2001.

Diane Dreher and Lao Tzu. *The Tao of Personal Leadership.* New York: HarperCollins, 1996.

Estes, Clarissa Pinkola. *Women Who Run With the Wolves.* New York: Ballantine, 1992.

Fox, Matthew. *Meditations with Meister Eckhart.* Sante Fe, NM: Bear & Co., 1983.

______*Original Blessing*. Santa Fe, NM: Bear & Co., 1984.

______*Reinvention of Work*. San Francisco, CA: Harper Collins, 1995.

______*Sins of the Spirit, Blessings of the Flesh.* New York: Harmony, 1995.

______*One River, Many Wells: Wisdom Springing from Global Faiths .* New York: Tarcher/Putnam, 2000.

______*Creativity: Where the Divine and Human Meet.* New York: Tarcher/ Putnam, 2002.

Grof, Stanislav and Christina. *Spiritual Emergency: When Personal Transormation Becomes a Crisis.* Los Angeles, CA: Tarcher, 1989.

Hanna, Thomas. *Somatics*. Menlo Park, CA: Addison-Wesley Pub, 1998.

Johanson, Greg and Kurtz, Ron. *Grace Unfolding: Psychotherapy in The Spirit of the Tao-Te Ching.* New York: Bell Tower, 1991.

Judith, Anodea and Vega, Selene. *The Sevenfold Journey.* Freedom, CA: The Crossing Press, 1993.

Kramer, Robert. "The Birth of Client-Centered Therapy: Carl Rogers, Otto Rank and 'the Beyond,'" in *Journal of Humanistic Psychology*, Vol. 35 N. 4, Fall, 1995, pp. 54-110.

Ladinsky, Daniel. *The Gift: Poems by Hafiz, the great Sufi master.* New York: Penguin/Putnam, 1999.

______*Love Poems from God.* New York: Penguin/Putnam, 2002.

Levine, Peter and Frederick, Ann. *Waking the Tiger: Healing Trauma: The Innate Capacity to Transform Overwhelming Experiences.* Berkeley, California: North Atlantic Books, 1997.

______*Healing Trauma: Restoring the wisdom of Your body.* Audiotape set, Denver, Co: Sounds True Recording, 1999.

______*In an Unspoken Voice.* Bekeley, CA: North Atlantic Books, 2010.

Malchiodi, Cathy. *The Soul's Palette.* Boston, MA: Shambhala, 2002.

Matt, Daniel. *The Essential Kabbalah: The Heart of Jewish Mysticism.* San Francisco: Harper, 1995.

McNiff, Shaun. *Art as Medicine: Creating a Therapy of the Imagination.* Boston, MA: Shambhala, 1992.

Mourier, Oona and Herriot, James. *The Nine Secrets to Bedroom Bliss.* Fairwinds Publishing, 2003.

Myss, Caroline. *Anatomy of Spirit The Seven Stages of Power and Healing.* New York: Harmony/Random House, 1996.

______*Sacred Contracts: Awakening your Divine Potential.* New York: Three Rivers Press, 2002.

Portia Nelson. *There's a Hole in My Sidewalk: The Romance of Self-Discovery.* Atria Books/Beyond Words, 1994.

Pascal, Eugene. *Jung to Live By: A Guide to the Practical Application of Jungian Principles for Everyday Life.* New York: Warner, 1992.

Pearson, Carol. *Awakening the Heroes Within.* San Francisco: Harper, 1991.

Pert, Candace B. *Molecules of Emotion.* New York: Scribner, 1997.

Pert, Candace, *Your Body is Your Subconscious Mind.* Audiotape. Denver, CO: Sounds True Recording, 2000.

Pugh, Meagan. *Somatic Art Therapy: Healing Body, Mind and Spirit.* Unpublished thesis, Sonoma State University, Rohnert Park, CA, 1994.

______*Finding a Safe Place in Your Body.* Audiotape, Sebastopol, CA. (self-published), 1998

______*Spiraling into Wholeness: A Practical Guide for Healing Using Creativity and Body Wisdom.* Unpublished dissertation. University of Creation Spirituality. Oakland, CA. 2004.

Rank, Otto. *Art and Artist.* New York: Norton. 1932, 1989.

______*Beyond Psychology*. New York: Dover Publications. 1941, 1958.

Rossi, Ernest L. *The Psychobiology of Mind-Body Healing: New Concepts of Therapeutic Hypnosis.* New York: W.W. Norton, 1987.

Rothschild, Babette. *The Body Remembers: the Psychophysiology of Trauma and Trauma Treatment.* New York: W.W. Norton, 2002.

Schneider, Michael. *A Beginner's Guide to Constructing the Universe: The Mathematical Archetypes of Nature, Art and Science.* New York: HarperCollins, 1994.

Swimme, Brian and Berry, Thomas. *The Universe Story* from the Primordial Flaring Forth to the Ecozoic Era—A Celebration of the Unfolding of the Cosmos. New York: HarperOne, 1994.

Wadeson, Harriet. *Art Psychotherapy*. New York: Wiley & Sons, 1980.

Whyte, David. *Fire in the Earth*. Langley, WA: Many Rivers Press, 1992.

______*The House of Belonging.* Langley, WA: Many Rivers Press, 1997.

______*Crossing the Unknown Sea.* New York: Riverhead Books, 2001.

Williamson, Marianne. *A Return to Love: Reflections on the Principles Of a Course in Miracles*. Chap. 7, Sec. 3. New York: Harper Collins, 1992.

INDEX OF CREATIVE PROCESSES

1. Beginning Self-Portrait
2. Finding a Safe Place in Your Body
3. Waking Up the Body Movement Exercise
4. Creating a Shield of Protection
5. Finding Your Inner Healer Guide
6. Sensing Your First Chakra Energy
7. Creating Your Little One
8. Torn-Paper Collage
9. Entering the Fruitful Dark
10. Empathetic Clay Process
11. Feeling Your Sensual Energy
12. Exploring Sexual Archetypes
13. Five Aspects of Self-Esteem
14. Exploring Personal Power
15. Self-Worth and Self-Critic
16. Entering the Realm of the Heart
17. Self-Forgiveness
18. Addictions
19. Exploring Your Throat Chakra
20. Sounding Exercises
21. Group Sounding
22. Yes/No Sounding
23. Core Beliefs
24. Visual Thinking
25. Conscious Prayer—An Exercise in Visioning
26. Animal Spirit Guide
27. Embodying the Ruler Archetype
28. Manifesting Your Inner Ruler – The Face of Sovereignty
29. Final Self-Portrait

INDEX OF FIGURES AND TABLES

Resources

Art Materials

Muslin blank dolls:

These are best found online at the following stores:

Sunshine Discount Crafts at http://www.sunshinecrafts.com/index.html orders@sunshinecrafts.com or This and That 4 You at sales@thisandthat4you.com

Portfolio oil pastels:

These are geared toward children but are very effective and have brilliant color. Find them in the children's department of most art supply stores.

Art and Craft supplies:

Feathers, glue, wooden sticks, jewels, paints, brushes, hot glue guns can all be found at Michaels Art Supply, Beverly's Crafts, Target, or a local craft store.

Papers:

Large papers are best found at art supply stores or at large chains where you can get good paper more reasonably. These are also available online at any art supply store. You have to pay for shipping, which adds to the price.

Miscellaneous materials:

Found at garage sales, recycle stores, end-of-season sales and companies that work with paper (printers, party stores).

Audio CDs

The following are examples of good background music for use during art-making, with the exception of *The Spiral of Healing* CD, which is used for the guided visualizations.

Berezan, Jennifer. *Returning. Albany, CA: Edge of Wonder Records,* 2000.
Evoking the lineage of ancient singing priestesses, this is a unique and beautiful blend of some of the world's most sacred musical traditions. Timeless and contemporary. Background music for moving and art.

Dolphina. *Music From The Goddess Workout.* Sea Siren Productions, Inc. 1998.
A high-energy, percussion instrumental CD that allows for stronger movement. A good choice for "waking up the body."

Enya. *A Day Without Rain.* Burbank, CA: Reprise Records, 2000.
Any of her CDs allow for relaxing background music, with a Celtic style, for imaginal process. Soothing and varied.

McFerrin, Bobby. *Circlesongs.* NYC: Sony Music Entertainment, 1996.
An improvisational acappella sound with many voices. Upbeat and jazzy. Can be used as background for art processes and for movement.

McKennitt, Loreena. *The Mask and Mirror.* Burbank, CA: Warner Bros. Records, 1994.
A dreamy celtic sound influence by Judaism, Islam, and Christianity. A spiritual blend of styles great for art process.

Parsons, David. *Ngaio Gamelan.* Tucson, Arizona: Celestial Harmonies (BMI).
A multicultural experience inspired by hundreds of fellow musicians from around the globe. Good as background for trance-like music for art.

Paul, Russill. *A.M./P.M. Yoga Chants.* The Relaxation Co., 2001
Transcendent chanting supported by rhythms and textures created by an evocative ensemble of Eastern and Western instrumentation. A.M. is more vigorous; P.M. more relaxing. Great for art and movement.

Premal, Deva. *The Essence* (1998) *and Love is Space* (2000). Boulder, CO:
White Swan Music.
Both of these CDs are full of contemporary, trance,
chanting music wonderful for movement and art process.

Roth, Gabrielle. *Endless Wave, Volume One* CD. Ravenrec@panix.com, 1996.
Wave I is a workout through the five rhythms. Wave II is an unguided tour through the five rhythms set to a percussion soundtrack. Track 1, Body Parts, is a good alternative to the basic "waking up your body" movement that appears throughout the book.

Pugh, Meagan. *Spiral of Healing CD.* Art to Heart Publications.
The Spiral of Healing CD contains guided visualizations for moving through the body via the chakras. Sold online at *www.art-2-heart.com.* Useful in conjunction with the book.

INDEX

D

E

F

H

I

K

L

M

N

O

P

Edwards Brothers Malloy
Thorofare, NJ USA
September 5, 2013